Dedicated

To

All the Past & Present Judges of the Supreme Court of India.

Salute to their wisdom.

Salute to their interpretation of Law.

Salute to their elaborative judgement writing.

• • •

COMPETITION & MONOPOLY MATTERS-SUPREME COURT'S LATEST LEADING CASE LAWS

CASE NOTES- FACTS- FINDINGS OF APEX COURT JUDGES & CITATIONS

JAYPRAKASH BANSILAL SOMANI

ISBN 979-888555828-0

Contents

Contents

Preface

Dear Learned Advocates of the Competition Commission, Competition Commission Appellate Tribunal, NCLAT, High Courts, Supreme Court, Corporates, Chartered Accountants, Consultants & Individuals

I am very delighted to provide you a book on 'Competition & Monopoly Matters- Supreme Court's Latest Leading Case Laws'.

In this book you will get...

1. Name of the Case i. e. Cause title

2.Relevant Sections discussed in the case

3. Hon'ble Judges/Coram of the case

4.Number of PDF Pages in Original Judgement of the case

5. All available Citations of the case

6. Case Note with appeal allowed/ dismissed or disposed off

7. Facts of the case

8. Hon'ble Apex Court's findings, while dismissing/allowing or disposing the appeal

9. Ratio Decidendi if any.

My special thanks to Manupatra, because of their web portal I can compile this book in well manner. I am also thankful to Notion Press to support me to publish & market this book throughout the Country. Thanks to my Juniors, Advocate Colleagues & Insolvency Professional Colleagues to support me in this venture.

Ms. Riya Srivastava has helped me a lot to compile this book.

I hope this book will add some value addition in the wealth of your legal knowledge. Your positive feedbacks will boost me to compile/ write further books & negative feedbacks will improve my skills. Kindly send your valuable feedbacks by email.

Thanks with Regards,

Jayprakash B. Somani

Advocate, Supreme Court of India

Email: jaysomani64@gmail.com

Web Site:www.jayprakashsomani.com

Call: 8384051134, 9322188701, 9318381287

• • •

Acknowledgements

Printed & Published by
Notion Press
No. 8, 3rd Cross Street,
CIT Colony, Mylapore,
Chennai, Tamil Nadu- 600004

• • •

Managed by
Jayprakash Somani Advocates & Solicitors
Law Firm for Supreme Court of India
Delhi Office
257 C, Pocket 1, Mayur Vihar Phase 1, Delhi 110091.
Call 8384051134, 9322188701, 8459194576, 9318381287
01141051516
Supreme Court Chamber
312, 3rd Floor, M. C. Setalvad Block, In front of 'D' Gate, Bhagwan Das Road, Supreme Court of India, New Delhi 110001
Contact: 8459194576, 9811011747,
www.jayprakashsomani.com

• • •

Books are available online at
1. **Notion Press:** https://notionpress.com/author/jayprakash_somani
2. **Amazon:** https://www.amazon.in/s?k=jayprakash+somani
3. **Flipkart:** https://www.flipkart.com/search?q=Jayprakash%20Somani

• • •

CHAPTER I

Competition Commission of India Vs. Bharti Airtel Limited and Ors. (05.12.2018)

Relevant Section:

Competition act, 2002 - section 26(1); competition act, 2002 - section 19(1)

Hon'ble Judges/Coram:

A. K. Sikri and Ashok Bhushan, JJ.

Equivalent Citation:2019(2)ABR56, AIR2019SC113, (2019)1CompLJ1(SC), I(2019)CPJ45(SC), (2019)2MLJ44, 2018(15)SCALE530, (2019)2SCC521, [2019]151SCL1(SC)

Number of pages in original judgment- 55

Case Note:

Anti-competitive agreement - Jurisdiction - Section 26(1) of Competition Act, 2002 - Present appeal was against order of Bombay High Court holding that, Competition Commission of India (CCI) had no jurisdiction in view of Telecom Regulatory Authority of India Act, 1997 and authorities and Regulations made thereunder; CCI could exercise jurisdiction only after proceedings under TRAI Act had concluded/attained finality - Whether writ petitions filed before High Court of Bombay were maintainable - Whether High Court could give its findings on merits.

Facts:

Reliance Jio Infocomm Limited ('RJIL') had filed information under Section 19(1) of Competition Act, 2002 before Competition Commission of India ('CCI') alleging anticompetitive agreement/cartel having been formed by three major telecom operators, namely, Bharti Airtel Limited, Vodafone India Limited and Idea Cellular Limited (Incumbent Dominant Operators) ('IDOs'). Apart from IDOs, certain allegations were also made against Cellular Operators Association of India ('COAI'). CCI issued notice to these parties and after hearing RJIL, aforesaid cellular companies and COAI, it passed a common order dated April 21, 2017 in all these cases (by clubbing them together) holding a view that, prima facie case existed and an investigation was warranted into matter. It, accordingly, directed Director

General to cause investigation in case. Four writ petitions came to be filed by Bharti Airtel Limited, Vodafone India Limited, Idea Cellular Limited and COAI respectively. prayed for quashing of aforesaid order and consequential action/proceedings on ground that CCI did not have any jurisdiction to deal with such a matter. Matter was heard and vide judgment dated September 21, 2017, High Court had allowed these writ petitions and quashed/set aside order dated April 21, 2017 passed by CCI and consequently notices issued by Director General of CCI had also been quashed. Bombay High Court in impugned judgment held that, Competition Commission of India (CCI) had no jurisdiction in view of Telecom Regulatory Authority of India Act, 1997 and authorities and Regulations made thereunder; CCI could exercise jurisdiction only after proceedings under TRAI Act had concluded/attained finality; Order dated 21st April, 2017 passed under Section 26(1) of Competition Act was not an administrative direction, but rather a quasi judicial one that finally decided rights of parties and caused serious adverse consequences, because a detailed hearing had been given and many materials had been tendered in courts of hearings; On merits of matter, there was no cartelisation as alleged and COAI was exonerated; and Order of CCI was perverse and liable to be interfered with under writ jurisdiction.

Held while dismissing the appeals:

1. Commission recognized role and importance of sectoral regulators and exercises its jurisdiction keeping in mind their role and responsibilities. Commission was a market regulator and had jurisdiction to look at those issues which affect competition in markets in India, including that of an alleged cartelization amongst enterprises/associations. nature of proceedings before TRAI involving ITOs on other hand different and related to whether interconnection norms and quality of service Regulations were complied with or whether contractual terms of ICAs had been breached or met. These issues were not relevant for determination in current proceedings before Commission. [11]

2. In wake of globalisation and keeping in view economic development of country, responding to opening of its economy and resorting to liberalisation, need was felt to enact a law that ensures fair competition in India by prohibiting trade practices which cause an appreciable adverse effect on competition within markets in India and for establishment of an expert body in form of Competition Commission of India, which would discharge duty of curbing negative aspects of competition, Competition

Act, 2002 had been enacted by Parliament. [65]

3. Functioning of telecom companies which were granted licence under Section 4 of Telegraph Act was regulated by provisions contained in TRAI Act. TRAI was a regulator which regulated telecom industry, which was a statutory body created under TRAI Act. [77]

4. Thus, with advent of globalisation/liberalisation leading to free market economy, regulators in respect of each sector had assumed great significance and importance. It becomes ir bounden duty to ensure that such a regulator fulfils objectives enshrined in Act under which a particular regulator was created. Insofar as telecom sector was concerned, TRAI Act itself mentions objective which it seeks to achieve. It not only exercised control/supervision over telecom service providers/licensees, TRAI was also supposed to provide guidance to telecom/mobile market. 'Introduction' to TRAI Act itself mentioned that due to tremendous growth in services it was considered essential to regulate telecommunication services by a regulatory body which should be fully empowered to control services, in best interest of country as well as service providers. [78]

5. TRAI was, thus, constituted for orderly and healthy growth of telecommunication infrastructure apart from protection of consumer interest. It was assigned duty to achieve universal service which should be of world standard quality on one hand and also to ensure that it was provided to customers at a reasonable price, on other hand. In process, purpose was to make arrangements for protection and promotion of consumer interest and ensure fair competition. It was because of this reason that powers and functions which were assigned to TRAI were highlighted in Statement of Objects and Reasons. Specific functions which were assigned to TRAI, amongst other, including ensuring technical compatibility and effective interrelationship between different service providers; ensuring compliance of licence conditions by all service providers; and settlement of disputes between service providers. [79]

6. In instant case, dispute raised by RJIL specifically touched upon these aspects as grievance raised was that IDOs had not given POIs as per licence conditions resulting into non-compliance and had failed to ensure inter se technical compatibility thereby. Not only RJIL had raised this dispute, it had even specifically approached TRAI for settlement of this dispute which had arisen between various service providers, namely, RJIL on one hand and IDOs on other, wherein COAI was also roped in. TRAI was seized of this particular dispute. [80]

7. TRAI was constituted as an expert regulatory body which specifically governed telecom sector, aforesaid aspects of disputes were to be decided by TRAI in first instance. These were jurisdictional aspects. Unless TRAI found fault with IDOs on aforesaid aspects, matter cannot be taken further even if we proceed on assumption that CCI had jurisdiction to deal with complaints/information filed before it. RJIL had approached DoT in relation to its alleged grievance of augmentation of POIs which in turn had informed RJIL vide letter dated September 06, 2016 that matter related to inter-connectivity between service providers was within purview of TRAI. RJIL thereafter approached TRAI; TRAI intervened and issued show-cause notice dated September 27, 2016; and post wassuance of show-cause notice and directions, TRAI issued recommendations dated October 21, 2016 on issue of inter-connection and provisioning of POIs to RJIL. Sectoral authorities were, therefore, seized of matter. TRAI, being a specialised sectoral regulator and also armed with sufficient power to ensure fair, non-discriminatory and competitive market in telecom sector, was better suited to decide aforesaid issues. After all, RJIL's grievance was that inter-connectivity was not provided by IDOs in terms of licenses granted to them. TRAI Act and Regulations framed reunder make detailed provisions dealing with intense obligations of service providers for providing POIS. These provisions also deal as to when, how and in what manner POIs were to be provisioned. They also stipulate charges to be realised for POIs that were to be provided to another service provider. Even consequences for breach of such obligations were mentioned. [83]

8. High Court was right in concluding that till jurisdictional issues were straightened and answered by TRAI which would bring on record findings on aforesaid aspects, CCI was ill-equipped to proceed in matter. Having regard to aforesaid nature of jurisdiction conferred upon an expert regulator pertaining to this specific sector, High Court was right in concluding that concepts of "subscriber", "test period", "reasonable demand", "test phase and commercial phase rights and obligations", "reciprocal obligations of service providers" or "breaches of any contract and/or practice", arising out of TRAI Act and policy so declared, were matters within jurisdiction of Authority/TDSAT under TRAI Act only. [84]

9. CCI was specifically entrusted with duties and functions, and in process empowered as well, to deal with aforesaid three kinds of anti-competitive practices. Purpose was to eliminate such practices which were having adverse effect on competition, to promote and sustain competition

and to protect interest of consumers and ensure freedom of trade, carried on by other participants, in India. To this extent, function that was assigned to CCI was distinct from function of TRAI under TRAI Act. Learned Counsel for Appellants were right in their submission that CCI was supposed to find out as to whether IDOs were acting in concert and colluding, thereby forming a cartel, with intention to block or hinder entry of RJIL in market in violation of Section 3(3)(b) of Competition Act. Also, whether there was an anti-competitive agreement between IDOs, using platform of COAI. CCI, therefore, was to determine whether conduct of parties was unilateral or it was a collective action based on an agreement. Agreement between parties, if it was there, was pivotal to issue. Such an exercise had to be necessarily undertaken by CCI. In Haridas Exports, this Court held that where statutes operate in different fields and had different purposes, it could not be said that there was an implied repeal of one by other. Competition Act was also a special statute which deals with anti-competition. If activity undertaken by some persons was anti-competitive and offended Section 3 of Competition Act, consequences thereof were provided in Competition Act. [89]

10. All aforesaid functions not only come within domain of CCI, TRAI was not at all equipped to deal with same. Even if TRAI also returned a finding that a particular activity was anti-competitive, its powers would be limited to action that could be taken under TRAI Act alone. It was only CCI which was empowered to deal with same anti-competitive act from lens of Competition Act. If such activities offend provisions of Competition Act as well, consequences under that Act would also follow. Therefore, contention of IDOs that jurisdiction of CCI stand totally ousted could not be accepted. Insofar as nuanced exercise from stand point of Competition Act was concerned, CCI was experienced body in conducting competition analysis. Further, CCI was more likely to opt for structural remedies which would lead sector to evolve a point where sufficient new entry was induced reby promoting genuine competition. This specific and important role assigned to CCI could not be completely wished away and 'comity' between sectoral regulator (i.e. TRAI) and market regulator (i.e. CCI) was to be maintained. [90]

11. Since matter pertained to telecom sector which was specifically regulated by TRAI Act, balance was maintained by permitting TRAI in first instance to deal with and decide jurisdictional aspects which can be more competently handled by it. Once that exercise was done and there

were findings returned by TRAI which lead to prima facie conclusion that IDOs had indulged in anti-competitive practices, CCI could be activated to investigate matter going by criteria laid down in relevant provisions of Competition Act and take it to its logical conclusion. This balanced approach in construing two Acts would take care of Section 60 of Competition Act as well. [91]

12. As per RJIL as well as CCI, High Court could not have entertained writ petition against an order passed under Section 26(1) of Competition Act which was a pure administrative order and was only a prima facie view expressed rein, and did not result in serious adverse consequences. [93]

13. Section 26, under its different Sub-sections, required Commission to issue various directions, take decisions and pass orders, some of which were even appealable before Tribunal. Even if it was a direction under any of provisions and not a decision, conclusion or order passed on merits by Commission, it was expected that same would be supported by some reasoning. At stage of forming a prima facie view, as required under Section 26(1) of Act, Commission might not really record detailed reasons, but must express its mind in no uncertain terms that, it was of view that prima facie case existed, requiring issuance of direction for investigation to Director General. Such view should be recorded with reference to information furnished to Commission. Such opinion should be formed on basis of records, including information furnished and reference made to Commission under various provisions of Act. Commission was expected to express prima facie view in terms of Section 26(1) of Act, without entering into any adjudicatory or determinative process and by recording minimum reasons substantiating formation of such opinion, while all its other orders and decisions should be well reasoned. [97]

14. Such an approach could also be justified with reference to Regulation 20(4), which required Director General to record, in his report, findings on each of allegations made by a party in intimation or reference submitted to Commission and sent for investigation to Director General, as case might be, together with all evidence and documents collected during investigation. Inevitable consequence was that, Commission was similarly expected to write appropriate reasons on every issue while passing an order under Sections 26 to 28 of Act. 15. Merely because present case dealt with telecom sector would not change nature of order that was passed by CCI under Section 26(1) of Competition Act. However, it raised another dimension. Even if order was administrative in nature, question raised before High

Court in writ petitions filed by Respondents touched upon very jurisdiction of CCI. As was evident, case set up by Respondents was that CCI did not have jurisdiction to entertain any such request or Information which was furnished by RJIL and two others. Question, thus, pertained to jurisdiction of CCI to deal with such a matter and in process High Court was called upon to decide as to whether jurisdiction of CCI was entirely excluded or to what extent CCI can exercise its jurisdiction in these cases when matter could be dealt with by another regulator, namely, TRAI. [96]

16. High Court was competent to deal with and decide issues raised in exercise of its power under Article 226 of Constitution. Writ petitions were, therefore, maintainable. [97]

17. Once it was held that, order under Section 26(1) of Competition Act was administrative in nature and further that it was merely a prima facie opinion directing Director General to carry investigation, High Court would not be competent to adjudge validity of such an order on merits. [98]

18. Since order of High Court was upheld on aspect that, CCI could exercise jurisdiction only after proceedings under TRAI Act had concluded/attained finality, i.e. only after TRAI returns its findings on jurisdictional aspects which were mentioned above, ultimate direction given by High Court quashing order passed by CCI was not liable to be interfered with as such an exercise carried out by CCI was premature. Appeals dismissed. [99]

• • •

CHAPTER II

Samir Agrawal Vs. Competition Commission of India and Ors. (15.12.2020)

Relevant Section:

Competition Act, 2002 - Section 3; Competition Act, 2002 - Section 45; Competition Act, 2002 - Section 53B; Competition Act, 2002 - Section 53N; Competition Act, 2002 - Section 53S; Competition Act, 2002 - Section 53T; Competition Act, 2002 - Section 2; Competition Act, 2002 - Section 18; Competition Act, 2002 - Section 19; Competition Act, 2002 - Section 26

Hon'ble Judges/Coram:

Rohinton Fali Nariman, K.M. Joseph and Krishna Murari, JJ.

Number of pages in original judgment- 18

Case Note:

MRTP/Competition Laws - Anti-competitive practices - Lack of - Sections 3, 3(1) and 3(3)(a) of Competition Act, 2002 - Appellant/ Informant, by Information filed sought that Competition Commission of India [CCI] initiate inquiry into alleged anti-competitive conduct of companies alleging that they entered into price-fixing agreements in contravention of Section 3(1) read with Section 3(3)(a) of Act, and engaged in resale price maintenance - Informant alleged that due to algorithmic pricing, neither were riders able to negotiate fares with individual drivers for rides that were booked through apps, nor were drivers able to offer any discounts - Therefore, Informant alleged that pricing algorithm used by companies artificially manipulates supply and demand, guaranteeing higher fares to drivers who would otherwise compete against one and another - CCI held that there was no contravention of provisions of Section 3 of Act and allegation as regards price discrimination also seems to be misplaced - Appellant/Informant, being aggrieved by Order of CCI, filed appeal before the National Company Law Appellate Tribunal (NCLAT) - NCLAT held that Informant had no locus standi to maintain action qua alleged contravention of Act and also rejected question of abuse of dominant position - Hence, present appeal - Whether alleged companies did facilitate cartelization or anti-competitive practices between drivers, so as to attract application of Section 3 of Act.

Facts:

The Appellant/Informant, by an Information filed sought that the Competition Commission of India (CCI) initiate an inquiry, under Section 26(2) of the Competition Act, 2002 into the alleged anti-competitive conduct of companies, alleging that they entered into price-fixing agreements in contravention of Section 3(1) read with Section 3(3)(a) of the Act, and engaged in resale price maintenance in contravention of Section 3(1) read with Section 3(4)(e) of the Act. The Informant alleged that due to algorithmic pricing, neither were riders able to negotiate fares with individual drivers for rides that were booked through the apps, nor are the drivers able to offer any discounts. Thus, the pricing algorithm takes away the freedom of riders and drivers to choose the best price on the basis of competition, as both have to accept the price set by the pricing algorithm. Therefore, the Informant alleged that the pricing algorithm used by companies artificially manipulates supply and demand, guaranteeing higher fares to drivers who would otherwise compete against one and another. The Competition Commission of India held that in the present case neither there appears to be any such agreement or meeting of minds between the Cab Aggregators and their respective drivers nor between the drivers inter-se. In result thereof, no contravention of the provisions of Section 3 of the Act appears to be made out given the facts of the present case. Further, the allegation as regards price discrimination also seems to be misplaced and unsupported by any evidence on record. The Appellant/Informant, being aggrieved by the Order of the CCI, filed an appeal before the National Company Law Appellate Tribunal. The NCLAT held that the Informant had no locus standi to maintain an action qua the alleged contravention of Act and also rejected the question of abuse of dominant position.

Held, while disposing off the appeal:

(i) Clearly, therefore, given the context of the Act in which the CCI and the NCLAT deal with practices which have an adverse effect on competition in derogation of the interest of consumers, it was clear that the Act vests powers in the CCI and enables it to act in rem, in public interest. This would make it clear that a person aggrieved must, in the context of the Act, be understood widely and not be constructed narrowly, as was done in Adi Pherozshah Gandhi. Further, it was not without significance that the expressions used in Sections 53B and 53T of the Act were any person, thereby signifying that all persons who bring to the CCI information of practices that were contrary to the provisions of the Act, could be said to be aggrieved by an adverse order of the CCI in case it refuses to act upon the information supplied. By way of contrast, Section 53N(3) speaks of making payment to an applicant as compensation for the loss or damage caused to the applicant as a result of any contravention of the provisions of Chapter II of the Act, having been committed by an enterprise. By this Sub-section, clearly, therefore, any person who makes an application for compensation, under Sub-section (1) of Section 53N of the Act, would refer only to persons who have suffered loss or damage, thereby, qualifying the expression any person as being a person who had suffered loss or damage. Thus, the preliminary objections against the Informant/Appellant filing Information before the CCI and filing an appeal before the NCLAT were rejected. [20]

(ii) The concurrent findings of fact of the CCI and the NCLAT, wherein it had been found that alleged companies did not facilitate cartelization or anti-competitive practices between drivers, who were independent individuals, who act independently of each other, so as to attract the application of Section 3 of the Act, as had been held by both the CCI and the NCLAT. Therefore, there was no reason to interfere with these findings. [23]

• • •

CHAPTER III

Competition Commission of India Vs. Thomas Cook (India) Ltd. and Ors.(17.04.2018)

Relevant Section:

Airports Economic Regulatory Authority Of India Act 2008, Competition Act, 2002, Electricity Act, 2003, Finance Act, 2017, Foreign Exchange Management Act, 1999 - Section 13; Income Tax Act, 1961

Hon'ble Judges/Coram:

Arun Mishra and Navin Sinha, JJ

Number of pages in the Original judgment- 11

Case Note:

Merger - Deletion of penalty - Challenge thereto - Sections 6(2) and 43 of Competition Act, 2002; Regulation 9(4) of SEBI (Substantial Acquisition of Shares and Takeovers) Regulations, 2011 - Whether Tribunal was right in setting aside order passed by Competition Commission whereby penalty of Rupees One Crore was imposed on Respondents on ground of non-compliance of provisions contained in Section 6(2) of Act?

Facts

2. The Thomas Cook India Ltd. (for short, "the TCIL") - Respondent No. 1, Thomas Cook Insurance Services India Limited, (for short, "the TCISIL") - Respondent No. 2 and Sterling Holiday and Resorts India Limited (for short, "the SHRIL") - Respondent No. 3 is the companies registered under the Companies Act, 1956. The TCIL is engaged in travel and travel related services. The TCISIL is also engaged in travel and travel related services and is a subsidiary of the TCIL and is also a registered corporate agent of Bajaj Allianz General Insurance Company Limited, which is engaged in the business of selling insurance to outbound travelers, as well as health insurance, motor insurance, personal accident insurance etc. SHRIL is engaged in the business of providing premium hotel services, vacation ownership services, normal hotel services like renting of rooms, restaurants, holiday activities etc. It also arranges meetings, incentives, conference and events for its corporate clients. The Board of Directors of the aforesaid three companies on 7.2.2014 approved a Scheme for demerger/amalgamation, (referred to as the 'Scheme'). The said Scheme contemplated the following:

(a) Demerger: i.e. Resorts and timeshare business of SHRIL were to be transferred by way of demerger from SHRIL to TCISIL in lieu of which equity shares of TCIL would be issued to shareholders of SHRIL as per the ratio in the 'Scheme'; and

(b) Amalgamation: SHRIL with its residual business would be amalgamated into TCIL in lieu of equity shares to be issued to the shareholders of SHRIL as per the ratio in the Scheme.

3. For the purpose of implementing the above transactions, the Respondents entered into a Merger Cooperation Agreement (for short, 'the MCA') on the same day i.e. on 07.2.2014.

4. On the very same day i.e. 07.2.2014, by another resolution of the Boards of Directors of the Respondents, the following transactions were approved and executed -

(i) Share Subscription Agreement (SSA): TCISIL was to subscribe 2,06,50,000 shares of SHRIL pursuant to a preferential allotment (amounting to 22.86% of SHRIL of equity share capital of SHRIL on fully diluted basis);

(ii) Share Purchase Agreement (SPA): TCISIL was to acquire 19.94% of equity share capital of SHRIL on the fully diluted basis from certain existing shareholders and promoters of SHRIL.

(iii) Open Offer by TCIL and TCISIL to purchase 26% of the equity share capital from public shareholders of SHRIL, in terms of the SEBI (Substantial Acquisition of Shares and Takeovers) Regulations, 2011 (in short, "the SEBI's Regulations").

5. In addition to the above, TCISIL acquired 90,26,794 equity shares of SHRIL through purchase on the Bombay Stock Exchange. These purchases (hereinafter referred to as "market purchases") amounted to 9.93% of the equity share capital of SHRIL on the fully diluted basis. The market purchases were made between 10.2.2014 and 12.2.2014.

6. On 14.2.2014, the Respondents sent a notice Under Section 6(2) of the Act to the Appellant - Commission, notifying only the 'Demerger' and 'Amalgamation'. Other transactions were, however, disclosed, while claiming exemption from Section 5 of the Act.

7. On 20.02.2014, the Commission asked the Respondents to remove certain defects in their application and provide further information, inter alia on, whether the notified and non-notified transactions were interrelated.

8. On 5.3.2014, the Commission passed an approval order Under Section 31(1) of the Act. However, it observed that the same would not affect the action proposed Under Section 43(A) of the Act for imposition of penalty in separate proceedings.

9. On 10.3.2014, the Commission issued a show cause notice asking the Respondents as to why they should not be penalized Under Section 43A for failing in notifying the 'market purchase' Under Section 6(2) of the Act.

10. On 25.3.2014, the Respondents filed their reply to the show cause. After hearing the Respondents, on 21.5.2014, the Commission imposed a penalty of Rupees One crore Under Section 43A of the Act. As against the same the appeal was preferred. The Tribunal has allowed the appeal filed Under Section 53B of the Act and has set aside the order passed by the Commission. Aggrieved thereby, the appeal has been preferred by the Commission Under Section 53B of the Act.

Held, while allowing the appeal:

Held, once a particular transaction or a series of transactions falls within purview of combination, it was obligatory to report same to Commission under Section 6 of Act. Section 6(1) prohibited combinations which cause or likely to cause an adverse effect on competition and such a combination shall be void. Section 6(2) of Act required that, advance notice had to be given of proposal to enter into a combination and that had to be given within 30 days of approval of proposal relating to merger or amalgamation, execution of any agreement or other document or acquisition referred to in Section 5(a) of Act. Section 6(2) made it clear that, no combination shall come into effect until 210 days had elapsed from the date on which notice had been given to Commission under Section 6(2) and Commission had passed orders under Section 30(1), whichever was earlier. It was apparent that, in notification made under Section 6(2) of Act, on 14th February, 2014 notifiable transactions were shown regarding merger and amalgamation. Parties had also contemplated certain other transactions in view of notifiable transaction, they were subscription of equity shares, SPA, open offer and market purchase. It was crystal clear from application itself that, all these transactions were part of same transactions and even before notifying transactions of purchase from market on 14th February, 2014, it was consummated between 10th February, 2014 to 12th February, 2014. All transactions were intrinsically connected and interdependent with each other and form part of one viable business transaction. Regarding exemption that, market purchases did not qualify as a combination in view of the target exemption notification which exempted an enterprise if 'assets' were of value not more than INR Rs. 250 crores in India or 'turnover' of not more than INR Rs. 750 crores in India. When series of transactions was envisaged to accomplish a combination, all transactions had to be taken into consideration by the Commission, not an isolated transaction. While it was open for parties to structure their transactions in a particular way the substance of transactions would be more relevant to assess effect on competition irrespective of whether such transactions were pursued through one or more step/transactions. Structuring of transactions could not be permitted in such a manner so as to avoid compliance with mandatory provisions of Act. Provision of Regulation 9(4) clearly acknowledged possibility of business transaction being inter-connected or inter-dependent steps of such transactions. Technical interpretation to isolate two different steps of transactions of a composite combination would be against spirit and provision of Act. Market purchases were not independent and could not be used in isolation for purpose of any exemption. Regulation 9(4) could not be interpreted to enable consummation by a composite combination before giving notice to Commission. Market purchases were part of same transaction of combination. Imposition of penalty under Section 43A of Act, was on account of breach of a civil obligation, and proceedings were neither criminal nor quasi-criminal; penalty had to follow. In the facts and circumstances of case, order passed by Commission was just and proper and in accordance with law, which Tribunal set aside on wrong premises. Nominal penalty had been imposed by Commission of Rupees One crore only considering facts and circumstances of case and that there was a violation of provision. Resultantly, appeal filed by Commission was allowed, order passed by Tribunal is set aside. Penalty of Rupees One crore was restored.

• • •

CHAPTER IV

Ultra Tech Cement Ltd. Vs. Competition Commission of India and Ors. (12.06.2013)

Relevant Section:

Competition Act, 2002 - Section 53T

Hon'ble Judges/Coram:

Gyan Sudha Misra and S.J. Mukhopadhaya, JJ.

Equivalent Citations- (2018)16SCC762

Number of pages in the Original Judgment- 5

Case Note:

MRTP/Competition Laws - Deposit of penalty - Condition thereto - Competition Commission imposed penalty on Appellants in view of allegation that Appellants had indulged in offence of cartelisation by creating artificial scarcity of cement in market in spite of their gross production, giving rise to artificial increase of price with sole intention to gain undue profit - Appellants challenged same by way of appeals before Competition Appellate Tribunal where appeals were subjudice - Tribunal while granting stay of payment of penalty imposed condition that Appellants shall pay ten percent of penalty to be deposited in Consolidated Fund of India and in event of non-payment by any Appellant, appeal of such Appellants shall stand dismissed - Hence, present appeal - Whether Tribunal erred in issuing direction to Appellants to deposit ten percent of amount of penalty imposed by Competition Commission.

Facts:

The Competition Commission imposed penalty on the Appellants in view of the allegation that the Appellants who were cement manufacturing companies had indulged in the offence of cartelisation by creating artificial scarcity of cement in the market in spite of their gross production, giving rise to artificial increase of price with a sole intention to gain undue profit. The Appellants challenged the same by way of appeals before the Competition Appellate Tribunal where the appeals were subjudice and the Tribunal while granting stay of payment of penalty imposed a condition that the Appellants shall pay ten percent of the penalty to be deposited in the Consolidated Fund of India and in the event of non-payment by any Appellant, the appeal of such Appellants shall stand dismissed.

Held, while disposing off the appeal:

(i) If the penalty order made by the CCI was not given effect to in a blanket way by exempting the Appellants from making the payment, it might practically amount to allowing their appeals by the Tribunal. Besides this, it was common practice in the legal arena that a decree, penalty or any order which was in the nature of payment in terms of money, the same was rarely interfered with and obviously so as in case of setting aside such order, the affected party could always be adequately compensated. At this stage, therefore, if the Tribunal thought it proper to take an equitable view of the matter by directing the Appellants to pay only ten percent of the amount to be paid by them, the same was not fit to be interfered with by way of an interim measure. The concern of this Court, however, was if the appeal was finally allowed by the Tribunal then what exactly would be the way out to pass on the amount of penalty to the benefit of the consumers, if the same was transferred to the State exchequer through the Consolidated Fund of India. [7]

(ii) Therefore, deem it appropriate to modify the order of the Tribunal to the extent that ten percent amount towards penalty be deposited with the Tribunal by each company and the Tribunal would ensure that a separate account was opened in a nationalised bank with a provision that the said amount was kept in a short term fixed deposit in the name of a company which will be initially for a period of six months renewable after the end of its expiry, if necessary. It goes without saying that the principal amount and the interest which was fetched by the account holders will be dealt with in the manner which would be considered appropriate by the Tribunal at the relevant stage of disposal of the appeals pending before it. [8]

• • •

CHAPTER V

SCM Solifert Limited and Ors. vs. Competition Commission of India (17.04.2018 - SC)

Relevant Section: Competition act, 2002 - section 6(2); competition act, 2002 - section 43a

Equivalent Citation:2018 4 AWC3364SC, 2018(5)BomCR75, 2018 (3) CCC 266 , 2018(4) CHN (SC) 291, [2018]144CLA15(SC), 2018CompLR417(Supreme Court), 2018 (3) CPR 480 , 2019-1-LW150, 2019(2)MhLj9, 2019(1)MPLJ521, 2018(6)SCALE38, (2018)6SCC631, 2018 (4) SCJ 576, [2018]147SCL273(SC)

Hon'ble Judges/Coram:

Arun Mishra and Navin Sinha, JJ.

Number of pages in the Original Judgment- 8

Case Note:

Merger - Acquisition of shares - Prior notice - Sections 6(2) and 43 of Competition Act, 2002 (Act)- Whether final judgment and order dated 30th August, 2016 passed by Competition Appellate Tribunal thereby affirming order passed by Competition Commission of India under Section 43A of Act was sustainable?

Facta

The Appellants SCM Solifert Limited and another are in appeal Under Section 53T of the Competition Act, 2002 (hereinafter referred to as "the Act") as against the final judgment and order dated 30.08.2016 passed in Appeal No. 59 of 2015 by the Competition Appellate Tribunal thereby affirming the order passed by the Competition Commission of India Under Section 43A of the Act.

2. The Competition Commission of India initiated the proceedings against the Appellants on whom due to the failure to notify a proposed combination as required Under Section 6(2) of the Act, the penalty of Rupees Two crores was imposed Under Section 43A of the Act. On 3.07.2013, the Appellants had purchased 2,89,91,150 shares of Mangalore Chemicals and Fertilisers Limited (in short referred to as "the MCFL") constituting 24.46 paid up share capital of the MCFL on the Bombay Stock Exchange.

3. The first transaction of the acquisition of the shares was by way of the purchase of shares conducted through bulk and block deals. It was followed by press release dated 3.7.2013 by Deepak Fertiliser and Petrochemicals Corporation Limited filed with the Stock Exchanges, in compliance with the requirements of the Listing Agreement.

4. On the second acquisition of the shares on 23.04.2014 the Appellants made a purchase order in the open market for the purchase of up to 20 lacs equity shares representing 1.7 percent shares of the MCFL. Subsequently, an open offer in terms of the SEBI (Substantial Acquisition of Shares and Takeovers) Regulations, 2011 (for short, "the Regulations, 2011") was made for acquiring up to 26 percent of shares of the MCFL.

5. The Appellants filed a notice disclosing details of the first acquisition and notifying the second acquisition Under Section 6(2) of the Act with the Commission on 22.04.2014 within thirty days of the public announcement pursuant to the Regulations, 2011 for the acquisition of 1.7 percent of the MCFL. The Competition Commission vide its order dated 30.07.2014 Under Section 31(1) of the Act approved the proposed combination, however, directed to initiate penalty proceedings against the Appellants Under Section 43A of the Act. Pursuant to that, a show cause notice was issued on the ground of failure to notify in accordance to Section 6(2) of the Act, in regard to first and second acquisitions of shares.

6. It was the case on behalf of the Appellants that first acquisition was made solely for the purpose of investment under Entry I of Schedule I of the CCI (Procedure in regard to the Transaction of Business Relating to Combinations) Regulations, 2011, (hereinafter referred to as "the Competition Regulations"). Thereby, it assumed exemption from the notification. It was also urged that the second acquisition was notified to the Commission within the stipulated time of 30 days as specified in Section 6(2) of the Act. The purchase was not consummated because as per the Escrow Agreement dated 28.04.2014, the shares purchased in the second acquisition were credited to a specifically designated Escrow account of J.M. Financial Services Limited. The sole purpose of entering into an escrow agreement was that the transaction was not consummated prior to approval of the Commission. The Commission has imposed the penalty of 2 crores; the appellate tribunal has affirmed the order. The Commission has held that the Appellants have violated Section 6(2) of the Act by failing to notify the proposed combination.

Held while dismissing the appeal

Held, it was apparent from Section 6(2) of Act that, proposal to enter into combination was required to be notified to Commission. Combination could not be entered into and shall come into effect before order was passed by Commission or lapse of certain time from date of notice is also apparent from terminology used in Section 6(2A) of Act, which provided that, no combination shall come into effect until 210 days have passed from date of notice or passing of orders under Section 31 of Act, by Commission, whichever was earlier. Notice of Section 6(2) of Act, was to be given prior to consummation of acquisition. Ex post facto notice was not contemplated under provisions of Section 6(2) of Act. Same would be in violation of provisions of Act. Factum of approval of combination subsequently by Commission was not going to provide an insulation, when provisions of Act had been violated and prior notice had not been given under Section 6(2) of Act. Provisions contained in Section 43A of Act, made it clear that, Commission shall impose penalty which might in its discretion extend to one per cent of total turnover or assets, whichever was higher, of combination. It had been found on facts that, turnover of combination was Rs. 3322 crores per annum, one per cent of which would be Rs. 33.22 crores. Commission had imposed a nominal penalty of Rs. 2 crores which amounted to only 0.06 per cent of total turnover. In facts of case, information was disclosed belatedly. Imposition of penalty was warranted due to violation of the provision and it was rightly imposed. There was no requirement of mens rea under Section 43A of Act or an intentional breach as an essential element for levy of penalty. Breach of provisions of Act was punishable and considering the nature of the breach, it is discretionary to impose extent of penalty. Imposition of penalty under Section 43A of Act, was on account of breach of a civil obligation, and proceedings were neither criminal nor quasi-criminal. Thus, a penalty had to follow. Discretion in provision under Section 43A was with respect to quantum. Thus, in view of submissions made by Appellants, no case for interference was made out. Appeal dismissed.

• • •

CHAPTER VI

Daulat Singh Rathore vs. Rajasthan Housing Board (04.12.2017 - SC)

Relevant Section:

Company law, mrtp and allied matters - matters pertaining to trai/sebi/idrai and rbi including appeals u/s 18 of trai act, indian elect act 1910 and 2003, elect supply act 1948 and elect reforms commn act 1998

Equivalent Citation: 2017 (4) CCC 497 , I(2018)CPJ4(SC), 2017(14)SCALE7, (2018)12SCC656

Hon'ble Judges/Coram:

Abhay Manohar Sapre and Navin Sinha, JJ.

Number of pages in the original judgment- 3

Facts

3. The Respondent herein is a State Housing Board (hereinafter referred to as "the Board"). The Board is constituted for the State of Rajasthan under the Rajasthan Housing Board Act, 1970 (hereinafter referred to as "the Act").

4. Pursuant to the Schemes introduced by the Board for sale of different types of Houses/flats in the city of Jodhpur, the Board invited applications from public at large in the year 1982 for sale of different categories of the houses/flats.

5. The Appellant made an application on 27.12.1982 (Annexure-P-1) to the Board for allotment of one flat to him at Jodhpur under a Scheme called, Middle Income Group "B" category. On 30.05.1983, the Appellant deposited a sum of Rs. 4,600/- as registration amount and then deposited a sum of Rs. 15,000/- on 18.09.1993 being first instalment.

6. Thereafter, there arose disputes between the Appellant and the Board for sale of the flat which, in the first instance, led to filing of the petition being Writ Petition No. 4707/1993 by the Appellant in the High Court of Rajasthan at Jodhpur. By order dated 04.05.1995, the High Court dismissed the writ petition as having rendered infructuous.

7. The Appellant then took recourse to two remedies for ventilating his grievance against the Board. He filed a suit being Civil Suit No. 23/2001 in the Court of ADJ(I) at Jodhpur on 02.07.2001 challenging therein the actions of the Board and simultaneously filed a complaint being UTPE No.

207/1998 before the MRTP Commission, New Delhi against the Board.

8. So far as the suit is concerned, it is still pending and so far as the complaint is concerned, it was dismissed by the MRTP Commission by impugned order dated 20.02.2006 giving rise to filing of this appeal by way of special leave by the Appellant in this Court. This Court granted leave on 17.05.2007.

9. On 11.08.2016, this Court recorded in the proceeding that the Appellant has given a proposal to the Board for reconsideration of his case for allotment of the flat. This Court observed that the Board should look into the Appellant's proposal with objectivity and call the Appellant personally to resolve the dispute out of the Court. On 19.10.2016, learned Counsel for the Respondent made a statement that the Board has decided to allot one flat to the Appellant and the details of the same would be placed on record within 2 weeks. On 23.03.2017, this Court wanted to find out the prices of the flats between 2005 to 2010. The Board has accordingly placed on record the details of the prices of the flats.

Held, while disposing the appeal

(i) The Board will allot one flat to the Appellant in Jodhpur in Board's Middle Income Group "B" Housing Scheme.

(ii) The Appellant will pay the price of the flat selected by him as per the approved Government's price prevalent and in force as on the date of this judgment.

(iii) The Board will adjust a sum of Rs. 19,600/- + interest @12% per annum to be calculated on Rs. 19,600/- from the date of its payment by the Appellant to the Board till the date of execution of sale deed by the Board in Appellant's favour from the total price and after giving adjustment of the said amount, i.e., (principal amount Rs. 19,600/- and interest) the balance would be considered as final price payable by the Appellant to the Board for purchase of flat.

(iv) In other words, the Appellant will pay a total price of the flat to the Board after deducting Rs. 19,600/- + interest to be calculated @ 12 % p.a. on Rs. 19,600/- from the date the said payment was made by the Appellant to the Board till the date of execution of sale deed of the flat.

(v) The Board will accordingly work out the price of the flat, as directed above, and inform the Appellant.

(vi) If the Appellant deposits the entire sale consideration, as directed above, within the time fixed by the Board in the notice sent to the Appellant, the Board will execute the sale deed in favour of the Appellant and also in favour of Appellant's first blood relation jointly along with the Appellant, in case, the Appellant expresses his wish to allow any of his blood relation to join with him as co-owner in execution of the sale deed. It is because it was stated at the bar that the Appellant is now quite aged. This liberty is, therefore, granted to the Appellant.

(vii) If the Appellant fails to pay the price within the time fixed by the Board then a sum of Rs. 19,600/- deposited by the Appellant with the Board shall stand forfeited.

(viii) Let all the formalities, as directed above, be completed within 6 months from the date of receipt of this judgment by the parties under intimation to both as an outer limit to give quietus to this litigation with no claim of any kind surviving against both the parties for future.

• • •

CHAPTER VII

Tata Engineering and Locomotive Company Ltd. vs. The Director (Research) on behalf of Deepak Khanna and Ors. (07.09.2015 - SC)

Relevant Section:

Monopolies and restrictive trade practices act, 1969 [repealed] - section 36

Equivalent Citation: 2015X AD (S.C.) 101, 2015(155)AIC267, 2015(6)ALLMR491, 2015 (6) AWC 5448 (SC), 2015(6)BomCR42, 2016(2)CDR532(SC), [2015]128CLA154(SC), 2015CompLR893(Supreme Court), (2015)4CompLJ161(SC), IV(2015)CPJ6(SC), 2016-3-LW242, 2016(1)RCR(Civil)56, 2015(4)RCR(Criminal)999, 2015(9)SCALE604, (2015)10SCC734, 2016 (1) SCJ 277, [2015]132SCL298(SC), 2016(1)UC344

Hon'ble Judges/Coram:

Vikramajit Sen and S.K. Singh, JJ.

Number of pages in the Original Judgment- 7

Facts

i) The practice under scrutiny is of the year 1999 when the Appellant was to begin the manufacture and delivery of newly introduced Tata Indica cars into the market with effect from February 1999, with the installed capacity of approximately 60,000 cars in a year. The Appellant invited the prospective customers to book the car through dealers. The booking amount demanded by the Appellant was quite high and close to the estimated price finally payable which would include excise duty, sales tax and transportation charges. The terms and conditions for booking of order for purchase of Tata Indica cars were mentioned in detail indicating the model wise price depending upon the city of booking. It was indicated that the price of vehicle as well as taxes, duties and cess will be as applicable on the date of delivery. Those making valid booking were to be supplied the vehicle as per priority numbers generated and allocated by a computerized technique, for the first 10,000 bookings only. The terms also provided that the payments against the remaining bookings will be refunded to the customers, without interest, at the earliest but in any case within a month from the closing of the booking. For refunds after a month, interest will be paid at the rate of 10% per annum. The order booking form mentioned in Clause 7 that the person concerned had carefully read the terms and conditions of the bookings and agreed to the same.

(ii) Although the initial allotment was confined only to 10,000 cars, the Appellant received as many as 1,13,768 booking applications along with stipulated amount which aggregated to Rs. 3,216.44 crores. The Appellant gave an option to prospective customers to opt for a second phase of 50,000 vehicles likely to be delivered from April-May 1999 to March 2000. It refunded the balance amounts to those who desired for refund, along with interest as represented. No complaint was made to the Commission by any of the persons who made the booking and thereafter either purchased the car or withdrew the deposits with or without interest, as the case may be.

(iii) However three complaints were made before the Commission by persons who claimed that they had intentions to make the booking but were dissuaded by the high quantum of deposit required for the purpose. Their specific objection was that the demanded amount exceeded the basic price of the car if cess, taxes and transportation cost were left out. According to the complainants the Appellant had indulged in Unfair Trade Practice (UTP) by demanding an excessive amount for bookings of Indica cars and by including the likely taxes, cess and transportation cost.

3. Since the defence taken by the Appellant was also not disputed on facts, it would be relevant to note the same. When the Commission received the three complaints, it sent them to the Director (Research) for investigation. The Director submitted Preliminary Investigation Reports (PIR) in all the three matters and three cases were registered as per numbers noted earlier. The Notices of Enquiry Under Sections 36-B (d), 37, 36-D of the Act and Under Regulation 51 were issued to the Appellant who contested the complaints.

Held while allowing the appeal

Held, Commission failed to keep in mind precise allegations against Appellant with a view to find out whether facts could satisfy definition of Unfair Trade Practice(s) as alleged against Appellant in Notice of Enquiry. Commission was apparently misled by Preliminary Investigation Report also, which claimed to deal with reply received from Appellant in course of preliminary enquiry but patently failed even to notice stipulation as regards to payment of interest on booking amount although this fact was obvious from terms and conditions of booking and was reportedly relied upon by Appellant in its reply even at the stage of preliminary investigation. Commission noticed relevant facts including provision for interest while narrating facts, but failed to take note of this crucial aspect while discussing relevant materials for the purpose of arriving at its conclusions. The order of the Commission appears to be largely influenced by a conclusion that the Appellant should not have asked for deposit of an amount above the basic price because in the opinion of the Commission it was unfair for the Appellants to keep excise and sales tax with itself for any period of time. Conclusion of Commission was based only upon subjective considerations of fairness and did not pass objective test of law as per precise definitions under Section 36A of Act. There was no scope to pass order under Section 36-D(1) of Act, when no case of any unfair trade practice was made out. Impugned order set aside. Appeal allowed.

• • •

CHAPTER VIII

A.B.N.A. and Ors. vs. The Managing Director, U.P.S.I.D.C. Limited, Kanpur and Ors. (08.05.2012 - SC)

Relevant Section:

Monopolies and Restrictive Trade Practices Act, 1969 [Repealed] - Section 13(2)

Equivalent Citation:2012(115)AIC121, AIR2012SC2007, [2012]110CLA384(SC), 2012(3)CLJ(SC)26, (2012)3CompLJ256(SC), (2012)3CompLJ256(SC), II(2012)CPJ1(SC), 2(2012)CPJ1(SC), 2013-1-LW228, 2012(3)RCR(Civil)682, 2012(5)SCALE256, (2012)12SCC618

Hon'ble Judges/Coram:

A.K. Patnaik and Swatanter Kumar, JJ.

Number of pages in the original judgment- 4

Facts

The facts very briefly are that the Respondents published an advertisement in the Hindustan Times, New Delhi inviting applications from entrepreneurs for allotment of industrial land in Greater NOIDA on payment of 10% of the cost of allotted land. In response to the advertisement, the Petitioners applied for a plot and on 05.03.1994 a plot of 800 square metres in Site-C was allotted. The Petitioners paid 10% of the cost of the plot on 23.03.1994. However, physical possession of the plot was not given to the Petitioners on the ground that the Petitioners had not paid all the dues for the plot. The Petitioners then filed a complaint UTPE No. 119 of 2000 before the MRTP Commission and after notice to the Respondents the complaint was heard from time to time. While the complaint was pending, Petitioners filed I.A. No. 18 of 2004 before the MRTP Commission to take possession of the allotted plot. On 13.09.2007, the MRTP Commission passed an order directing that the Respondent shall handover possession of the allotted plot within next two weeks to the complainant and as regards the balance amount, if any due, the Respondents shall submit a detailed chart giving the dates on which the subsequent installments were due and the amount payable on each due date. By the order dated 13.09.2007, the MRTP Commission also directed the Petitioners to furnish a fresh SSI certificate to the Respondents and directed that the matter be listed on 01.11.2007 for further directions. Instead of handing over possession of the allotted plot to the Petitioners, the Respondents filed Review Application No. 16 of 2007 on 18.12.2007 and by the impugned order dated 04.03.2009 the MRTP Commission allowed the Review Application and recalled the order dated 13.09.2007 insofar as it directed the Respondents to handover possession of the plot to the Petitioners. Aggrieved, the Petitioners filed Review Application No. 06 of 2009 before the Competition Appellate Tribunal and by the impugned order dated 05.01.2010, the Competition Appellate Tribunal dismissed the Review Application of the Petitioners.

Held while dismssing the appeal

6. It is not disputed by the Petitioners that Review Application No. 16 of 2007 was entertained by the MRTP Commission under Sub-section (2) of Section 13 of the MRTP Act. Sub-section (2) of Section 13 of the MRTP Act is quoted hereinbelow:

13(2) Any order made by the Commission may be amended or revoked at any time in the manner in which it was made.

The language of Sub-section (2) of Section 13 makes it clear that the MRTP Commission may amend or revoke any order in the manner in which it was made "at any time". The expression "at any time" would mean that no limitation has been prescribed by the legislature for the MRTP Commission to amend or revoke an order passed by it. Hence, the argument on behalf of the Petitioners that the MRTP Commission could not have entertained the Review Application for recalling the order dated 13.09.2007 beyond the period of 30 days has no foundation in law. Moreover, the order dated 13.09.2007 of the MRTP Commission on its plain reading was only an interim order and the MRTP Commission could modify or revoke the interim order directing the Respondents to handover physical possession of the plot to the Petitioners if it thought that such a direction could only be considered at the time of finally deciding the complaint. We therefore do not find any infirmity in the order dated 04.03.2009 of the MRTP Commission recalling the direction to handover physical possession of the allotted plot to the Petitioner saying that this direction can be considered at the stage of final adjudication of the complaint.

7. On a perusal of the impugned order dated 04.03.2009, however, we find that although the Respondents cited the judgment of this Court in

Ghaziabad Development Authority v. Ved Prakash Aggarwal (supra) and contended before the MRTP Commission that the MRTP Commission had no authority to order handing over of possession and that the jurisdiction was only with the Civil Court to order specific performance of the contract, the MRTP Commission has observed that this contention cannot be dealt with while passing the interim order and can only be decided at the time of final adjudication of the complaint. Hence, we are not called upon to decide the question whether the MRTP Commission has power to direct handing over the possession of the plot to the complainant and this question can be decided by the MRTP Commission at the stage of final adjudication of the complaint.

8. In the result, we do not find any merit in these Special Leave Petitions and accordingly we decline to grant special leave to the Petitioners to appeal against the order dated 04.03.2009 of the MRTP Commission and the order dated 05.01.2010 of the Competition Appellate Tribunal. The Special Leave Petitions are dismissed with no order as to costs.

• • •

CHAPTER IX

Colgate Palmolive (India) Ltd. vs. M.R.T.P. Commission and Ors. (20.11.2002 - SC)

Relevant Section:

Monopolies And Restrictive Trade Practices Act, 1969 [repealed]

Equivalent Citation: AIR2003SC317, 2003(1)ALLMR(SC)773, (2003)2CALLT28(SC), [2002]51CLA285(SC), [2003]113CompCas14(SC), (2003)1CompLJ36(SC), (2003)1CompLJ213(SC), (2003)1CompLJ213(SC), (2003)1CompLJ36(SC), III(2002)CPJ18(SC), IV(2015)CPJ13(SC), JT2002(9)SC464, 2003(1)RCR(Civil)74, 2002(8)SCALE507, (2003)1SCC129, [2003]41SCL98(SC), 2003(1)UJ31

Hon'ble Judges/Coram:

G.B. Pattanaik, C.J. and S.B. Sinha, J.

Number of pages in the original judgment - 5

Facts

The appellant had inserted an advertisement in several newspapers in September, 1984 announcing a contest known as "Colgate Trigard Family Good Habits Contest". 'Trigard' is the name of tooth brush manufactured by the appellant. By reason of the said advertisement, a contest apparently for the purpose of educating the families for inculcating good habit of taking care of dental health was announced.

The brief particulars of the contest are as under:-

As a condition precedent to participating in the contest each prospective participant was required to send two upper portion of the cartons in which the Trigard Tooth-brushes were sold. These two upper portions of the carton were to be sent along with each entry form which was required to bear the dealers' name and address duly rubber-stamped on the form. Obviously this necessitated the purchase of two Trigard Colgate brushes by a prospective participant in the contest. The entry form contained four questions, each with two alternative answers which were also printed. The contestant was required to tick mark the correct answer.

Anyone with an ordinary knowledge of dental health could tick mark the correct answer to those questions. But this was not enough. In addition to answering the questions as mentioned above, each contestant had to write a sentence not exceeding ten words describing as to why the contestant's family used Colgate Trigard Tooth-brush. The best entry in this regard would win the first prize. There were several other prizes for second, third and fourth winners. In all there were fifty prizes.

8. Appellant further offered 825 consolation prizes of Rs. 100/- each and 1200 early bird prizes of Rs. 50/- each to be awarded to those 100 entries which were received first every week. The last mentioned prizes were irrespective of whether the answers to the questions were correct or not and irrespective of the merit of the slogan which was to be provided by the contestant.

9. A complaint was made to the Commission alleging that the said contest which was organised by the appellant for the purpose of promotion or sale of its product was in its own interest and prejudicial to the interest of the consumer generally as a result whereof serious injury or loss to the consumer concerned was caused. The complainant alleged that such contests fell within Clause (b) of paragraph 3 of Section 36A of the M.R.T.P. Act.

10. On receipt of the said complaint an investigation was directed to be made, pursuant whereto and in furtherance whereof upon an enquiry, a preliminary investigation report was submitted by the Director General who also came to the conclusion that the said contest was covered by Section 36A(3)(b) of the M.R.T.P. Act.

Held, while setting aside the appeal

19. Causation of loss or injury thus is a sine qua non for invoking the principles of Section 36A of the M.R.T.P. Act. The Commission, in our considered opinion, committed a manifest error in holding that the actual loss or injury is not an essential ingredient of the unfair trade practice.

20. It is now a well-settled principle of law that a literal meaning should be assigned to a statute unless the same leads to anomaly or absurdity. The terminology used in the provisions is absolutely clear and unambiguous. As noticed hereinbefore, in terms of the aforementioned provisions not only a trade practice is resorted to for the purpose of promoting sale or use or supply of any goods or service, as specified therein but thereby loss or injury to the consumers of such goods or services must be caused. The word 'thereby' must be assigned its plain meaning for interpreting of the aforementioned provision.

21. In H.M.M. Ltd.'s case (supra), this Court has clearly held that for holding a trade practice to be an unfair trade practice, it must be found that

it had caused loss or injury to the consumer.

22. We may notice that on or about 1993 an amendment has been made whereby the words "causing loss or injury to the consumer" were omitted which also goes to show the law as it stood thence, 'loss or injury to the consumer' was a pre-requisite for attracting the provisions of Section 36A(3)(b) of the Act.

23. In interpreting the said provision, the "Mischief Rule" should be resorted to.

24. For the view, we have taken, the impugned judgments cannot be sustained, which are set aside accordingly. The appeals are allowed but in the facts and circumstances of the case there will be no order as to costs.

• • •

CHAPTER X

Manjeet Kaur Monga (Dead) thr. her Legal Heirs Karan Vir Singh Monga Vs. K.L. Suneja and Ors (18.07.2017)

Relevant Section: Monopolies and Restrictive Trade Practices Act, 1969 [Repealed] - Section 12B; Monopolies and Restrictive Trade Practices Act, 1969 [Repealed] - Section 36 A

Equivalent Citation: 2018(1)JCC95, 2017(4)RCR(Civil)425, 2017(8)SCALE308, (2018)14SCC679

Hon'ble Judges/Coram:

Kurian Joseph and R. Banumathi, JJ.

Number of pages in the original document- 6

Case Note:

MRTP/Competition Laws - Compound interest - Entitlement thereto - Section 36-A of Monopolies and Restrictive Trade Practices Act, 1969 - Competition Appellate Tribunal held that Respondents not only failed to complete project within stipulated time but also failed to return installments deposited by the Complainant - It was declared that the Respondents had acted in violation of Section 36-A(1) (i), (ii) and (ix) of Act and they were guilty of unfair trade practice, Respondents were directed to pay compound interest to the Legal Representatives/Appellant of Complainant - Interest should be calculated on each instalment paid by other person and Complainant from date of deposit - Hence, present appeal - Whether Appellant should be entitled to compound interest from original dates of payment.

Facts:

Competition Appellate Tribunal held that Respondents not only failed to complete the project within the stipulated time but also failed to return the installments deposited by the Complainant. It was declared that the Respondents had acted in violation of Section 36-A(1) (i), (ii) and (ix) of the Act and they were guilty of unfair trade practice, the Respondents were directed to pay compound interest to the legal representatives of the Complainant. The interest should be calculated on each instalment paid by other person and the Complainant from the date of deposit. Hence, present appeal.

Held, while disposing off the appeal:

(i) The amount referred to under the Section was the amount at fifteen percent compound interest on the amount already deposited, as ordered by the Tribunal. Merely, because a liquidated amount was not stipulated or determined by the Tribunal, it could not be said that it was not the compensation. Once the interest, as ordered by the Tribunal, was calculated that would be the amount of compensation referred to under Section 12B of the Act. [5]

(ii) It could not be said that the money was enjoyed by the Bank, since being a pay order, at any moment the instrument was presented, the Bank was bound to honour the same and, therefore, only for the lapse on the part of either the payee or the account holder for encashing or cancelling the instrument, the Bank could not be saddled with any interest. Matter remitted back to the Competition Appellate Tribunal for limited purpose. [7] and[9]

• • •

CHAPTER XI

Rajasthan Cylinders and Containers Limited Vs. Union of India (UOI) and Ors.(01.10.2018)

CCompetition act, 2002 - section 3(3)(d); competition act, 2002 - section 27

Hon'ble Judges/Coram:

A.K. Sikri and Ashok Bhushan, JJ.

Equivalent Citation: 2018 (4) CCC 376 , 2018 (4) CPR 647 , (2019)1MLJ601, 2018(13)SCALE493, (2020)16SCC615, 2019 (4) SCJ 247, [2018]150SCL1(SC)

Number of pages in the original document- 39

Case Note:

MRTP/Competition Laws - Cartelisation - Imposition of penalty - Sections 3(3)(a), 3(3)(d) and 27 of Competition Act, 2002 - Competition Commission of India (CCI) held that Appellants/suppliers of Liquefied Petroleum Gas (LPG) Cylinders to public sector company had indulged in cartelisation, thereby influencing and rigging prices, thus, violating provisions of Section 3(3)(d) of Act - CCI, as result, imposed severe penalties in form of fines under Section 27 of Act - On appeal, Competition Appellate Tribunal, while maintaining order of CCI insofar as it found Appellants guilty of contravention of Section 3(3)(d) and also under Section 3(3)(a) of Act, Appellate Tribunal had reduced amount of penalty - Hence, present appeal - Whether Appellants had indulged in cartelisation, thereby influencing and rigging prices, thus, violating provisions of Section 3(3)(d) of Act.

Facts:

The Appellants were manufacturing gas cylinders of a particular specification which were needed for use by the three oil companies in India. The suo-motu proceedings were started by the CCI on the basis of the information received by it in Case No. 10 of 2010 titled M/s. Pankaj Gas Cylinders Ltd. v. Indian Oil Corporation Ltd. in that case a complaint was made before the CCI complaining about unfair conditions in the tender floated by oil company. The Competition Commission of India that the Appellants/suppliers of Liquefied Petroleum Gas (LPG) Cylinders to the public sector company had indulged in cartelisation, thereby influencing and rigging the prices, thus, violating the provisions of Section 3(3)(d) of the Competition Act, 2002. The CCI, as a result, imposed severe penalties in the form of fines under Section 27 of the Act. While maintaining the order of the CCI insofar as it found the Appellants guilty of contravention of Section 3(3)(d) and also under Section 3(3)(a) of the Act, the Competition Appellate Tribunal had reduced the amount of penalty.

Held, while allowing the appeal:
(i) Monopsony consists of a market with a single buyer. When there were only few buyers the market was described as an oligopsony. What was emphasised was that in such a situation a manufacturer with no buyers would have to exit from the trade. Therefore, first condition of oligopsony stands fulfilled. The other condition for the existence of oligopsony was whether the buyers have some influence over the price of their inputs. It was also to be seen as to whether the seller has any ability to raise prices or it stood reduced/eliminated by the buyers. [94]

(ii) The Appellants had been able to discharge the onus by referring to various indicators which go on to show that parallel behaviour was not the result of any concerted practice. [95]

(iii) The inferences drawn by the CCI on the basis of evidence collected by it are duly rebutted by the Appellants and the Appellants had been able to discharge the onus that shifted upon them on the basis of factors pointed out by the CCI. However, at that stage, the CCI failed to carry the matter further by having required and necessary inquiry that was needed in the instant case. [101]

(iv) There was no sufficient evidence to hold that there was any agreement between the Appellants for bid rigging. Accordingly, set aside the order of the Authorities below. As a consequence, no penalty was payable. [103]

• • •

CHAPTER XII

Union of India (UOI) and Ors. vs. Hindustan Development Corpn. and Ors. (15.04.1993 - SC)

Relevant Section: Monopolies and Restrictive Trade Practices Act, 1969, Constitution Of India

Equivalent Citation: AIR1994SC988, (1993)2CompLJ171(SC), (1993)2CompLJ171(SC), JT1993(3)SC15, 1993(2)SCALE506, (1993)3SCC499

Hon'ble Judges/Coram:

K. Jayachandra Reddy and G.N. Ray, JJ

Number of pages in the original judgment- 32

Facts

Every year the Railway Board enters into contracts with the manufacturers for the supply of cast steel bogies which are used in turn for building the wagons. Cast steel bogies come under a specialised item procured by the Railways from the established sources of proven ability. There are 12 suppliers in the field who have been regularly supplying these items. Two new firms Simplex and Beekay also entered the field. Among them admittedly M/s. H.D.C., Mukand and Bhartiya are bigger manufacturers having, capacity to manufacture larger quantities. On 25.10.91 a limited tender notice for procurement of 19000 cast steel bogies was issued to the regular suppliers as well as the above two new entrants for the year namely from 1.4.92 to 31.3.93. The last date for submission of offers to the Ministry of Railways was 27.11.91 by 2,30 P.M. and the tenders were to be opened on the same day at 3 P.M. It was also stated therein that the price was subject to the price variation clause and the base date for the purpose of escalation was 1.9.91 and that the Railways reserved the right to order additional quantity up to 30% of the ordered quantity during the currency of the contract on the same price and terms and conditions with suitable extensions in delivery period. The offers were to remain open for a period of 90 days. On that day the tenders were opened in the presence of all parties. The price quoted by the three manufacturers i.e. M/s. H.D.C, Mukand and Bharatiya was an identical price of Rs. 77,666/- per bogie while other tenderers quoted between 83,0007- and 84,500/- per bogie. After the tenders were opened and before the same could be finalised, the

Government of India announced two major concessions namely reduction of custom duty on the import of steel scrap and disposition of freight equalisation fund for steel. The tenders were put up and placed before the Tender Committee of the Railways which considered all the aspects. The Committee concluded that three of the tenderers namely M/s. H.D.C., Mukand and Bhartiya who had quoted identical rates without any cushion for escalation between 1.7.92 and 1.9.91, have apparently formed a cartel. The Tender Committee also noted that the rates quoted by them were the lowest. Taking into consideration the reduction of Rs. 1500/- as a result of the concessions in respect of the reduction of customs duty on the import of steel scrap and dispensation of the freight equalisation fund for steel, the Tender Committee concluded that the reasonable rate would be Rs. 76,000/- per bogie. On the question of distribution of quantities to the various manufacturers the Tender Committee decided to follow the existing procedure the Tender Committee signed these recommendations on 4.2.92 but on the same day the Member (Mechanical) of the Committee received letters from M/s. H.D.C. and Mukand. M/s. H.D.C. in its letter stated that in view of the concessions and also on the basis that per Kg. rate of Casting per bogie could be reduced from Rs. 37.50 to Rs. 29/- the Cost of casting can also be reduced and therefore they would be in a position to supply the bogies at a lesser rate, in case a negotiation meeting is called. M/s. Mukand in its letter also offered to substantially reduce the prices and they would like to co-operate with the Railways and the Government and bring down the prices as low as possible and asked for negotiations. Though this was post-tender correspondence, the Department felt that the first insistence and by M/s. H.D.C. and Mukand could b considered. The whole matter was examined by the Advisor (Finance)in the offers made by an elaborate note he observed that the need for encouraging open competition to improve quality and bring down costs has been recommended by the Government and if it is intended to continue the existing policy of fixing a rate and distributing the order among all the manufacturers, then negotiations may not be useful as uniform prices offered to all manufacturers have to be sufficient even for the smaller and less economical units and that as any review of the existing policy would take time, the present tender can be decided on the basis of the existing policy. With this noting the file was immediately sent to the Member (Mechanical), the next higher authority. He, with some observations, however recommended the acceptance of the Tender Committee's recommendations. The file was then put up to

Financial Commissioner. He noted that the Tender Committee was convinced that the three manufacturers who quoted identical price of Rs. 77,666/- had formed a cartel. He also considered the offers made by H.D.C. and Mukand and observed that these three manufacturers who quoted a cartel price intended to get a larger order on the basis of such negotiated price which would eventually nullify the competition from the other manufacturers and lead to their industrial sickness and subsequently to monopolistic price situation. He, however, approved the Tender Committee's recommendations that a counter-offer of Rs. 76,000/- may be accepted but in the case of M/s. H.D.C. a price lower by Rs. 11,000/- may be offered as per their letter dated 4.2.92. He also recommended that the two manufacturers M/s. Cimmco and Texmaco may be given orders to the extent of their capacity or quantity offered by them whichever is lower in view of the fact that they are wagon builders and the present formula regarding the distribution of quantities may be applied to all manufacturers except the three who have formed a cartel. He also recommended some recoveries from these three manufacturers who are alleged to have formed a cartel on the basis of their letters wherein they have quoted prices which were much less than the updated price as on 1.9.91 of Rs. 79,305/-. He also made certain other recommendations and finally concluded that the post-tender letters may be ignored and that for short-term gains the Department can not sacrifice long-term healthy competition. After these recommendations of the Financial Commissioner the file was put up to the approving authority i.e. the Minister for Railways, who in general agreed with the recommendations of the Financial Advisor. He also noted that these three manufacturers have formed a cartel. He also noted that subsequent to the Financial Commissioner's note, besides M/s. H.D.C. and Mukand has also offered to reduce the price by 10% or more vide their letter dated 19.2.92 if called for negotiations. Taking these circumstances into consideration the Minister ordered that all these three firms may be offered a price lower by Rs. 11,000/- with reference to the counter-offer recommended by the Tender Committee and the quantities also be suitably adjusted so that the cartel is broken. The Minister also noted that as a result of this a saving of about Rs. 11 crores would be effected. In his note, the Minister also ordered redistribution of the quantities. He also ordered that 30% option should straightaway be exercised. After the approving authority took these decisions, the file went to the Chairman, Railway Board for implementing the decisions. He noted that action will be taken as decided by the Minister but added that it results in dual-pricing namely one to the three manufacturers and the higher one to the others and therefore the Minister may consider whether they could counter-offer the lower price to all the manufacturers as that would result in saving much more. The file was then again sent to and was considered by the Financial Commissioner who noticed this endorsement made by the Chairman, Railway Board. He however noted that so far all the other firms are concerned it is Rs. 3305/- less than the present contract price but it would not be equitable to offer the lower price put forward by the three manufacturers as it would make the other units unviable and that incidentally the price of Rs. 76,000/- now proposed to be counter-offered to the other firms is also in line with the recommendations of the Tender Committee. He, however, noted that some of the units were sick units and owe a lot of money to the nationalised banks and it would therefore be in the national interest to accept dual-pricing. therefore the file was again put up to the approving authority who agreed with the recommendations of the Financial Commissioner and the Tender Committee and directed that the same may be implemented. In view of this final decision taken by the approving authority a telegram was issued to the three manufacturers giving them a counter-offer of Rs. 65,000/- per bogie. The counter-offer was also made to the other nine manufacturers at the rate of Rs. 76,000/- per bogie namely the price worked out by the Tender Committee. Soon after the receipt of this telegram dated 18.3.92 M/s. H.D.C. and Mukand filed writ petitions in the Delhi High Court challenging the so-called discriminatory counter-offer. M/s. Bharatiya also filed a similar petition in Calcutta High Court but the same was withdrawn but another writ petition was filed later in Delhi High Court. In the writ petitions filed by M/s. H.D.C. and Mukand, the High Court stayed the operation of the telegram dated 18.3.92 and issued notice to the Union of India and to the Executive Director and Director of the Railways (Stores) who figured as respondents in those writ petitions. M/s. H.D.C. and Mukand also wrote to the Minister of Railways in reply to the telegram that they were not prepared to accept to the counter-offer at the rate of Rs. 65,000/- and instead they offered to supply the bogies at the rate of Rs. 67,000/- per bogie. The Railways accepted this offer and intimated M/ s H.D.C. and Mukand accordingly. The High Court, at an interlocutory stage pending the writ petitions, passed an order on 2.4.92 directing the Ministry to accept the allocation of bogies recommended by the Tender Committee and to pay a price at the rate of Rs. 67,000/- only per bogie and that would be subject to the final decision of the writ petitions. Being aggrieved by this order, the Railways filed a petition for special leave to appeal Rs. 5512/92 and this Court while refusing to interfere at that interlocutory stage made the following observations on 28.4.92:

However, we may observe...and so direct...that during the pendency of the writ petition if any of the supplies in terms of the package of distribution indicated by the High Court (including the petitioners in the High Court) in the writ petition) seek an "on-account" payment representing the difference between the sum of Rs. 67,000/-indicated as price by the High Court and the sum of Rs. 76,000/- contemplated by the Railways; the order of the High Court shall not prohibit the Government making such on-account payment to such suppliers on each wagon on the condition that the said on-account payment of Rs. 9,000/- per bogie should be covered by a bank guarantee for its prompt repayment together with interest at 20% per annum in the event the on-account payment cannot be observed in the price structure that may ultimately come to be determined pursuant to the final decision in the writ petitions. The special leave petitions are disposed of accordingly.

HELD

On examination of some of these important decisions it is generally agreed that legitimate expectation gives the applicant sufficient locus standi for judicial review and that the doctrine of legitimate expectation is to be confined mostly to right of a fair hearing before a decision which results in negativing a promise or withdrawing an undertaking is taken. The doctrine does not give scope to claim relief straightaway from the administrative authorities as no crystalised right as such is involved. The protection of such legitimate expectation does not require the fulfillment of the expectation where an overriding public interest requires otherwise. In other words where a person's legitimate expectation is not fulfilled by taking a particular decision then decision-maker should justify the denial of such expectation by showing some overrating public interest. therefore even if substantive protection of such expectation is contemplated that does not grant an absolute right to a particular person. It simply ensures the circumstances in which that expectation may be denied or restricted. A case of legitimate expectation would arise when a body by representation or by past practice aroused expectation which it would be within its powers to fulfill. The protection is limited to that extent and a judicial review can be within those limits. But as discussed above person who bases his claim on the doctrine of legitimate expectation, in the first instance, must satisfy that there is a foundation and thus has locus standi to make such a claim. In considering the same several factors which give rise to such legitimate expectation must be present. The decision taken by the authority must be found to be arbitrary, unreasonable and not taken in public interest. If it is a question of policy, even by way of change of old policy, the courts can not interfere with a decision. In a given case whether there are such facts and circumstances giving rise to a legitimate expectation, it would primarily be a question of fact. If these tests are satisfied and if the court is satisfied that a case of legitimate expectation is made out then the next question would be whether failure to give an opportunity of hearing before the decision affecting such legitimate expectation is taken, has resulted in failure of justice and whether on that ground the decision should be quashed. If that be so then what should be the relief is again a matter which depends on several factors

In view of our conclusions in respect of the quantagarwalities allotted and the price fixed it may not be necessary for us to enter into further discussion on this aspect. We have already directed that the Tender Committee should consider afresh as to what should be the reasonable price and to that extent the price of Rs. 67,000/- fixed in respect of smaller manufacturers is set aside and directed to be revised. So far these three big manufacturers are concerned, we held that on their own commitment they are bound to supply at the rate of Rs. 67,000/- per bogie. So far the quantities are concerned, we held that these three big manufacturers should be allotted the quantities as per the recommendations of the Tender Committee. However, we considered this aspect to some extent only to show that the decision in respect of price fixation as well as allotment of quantities even though to some extent at variation with the procedure followed during the previous years, was not based on any irrelevant consideration. The Railways particularly the Financial Commissioner as well as the Minister and initially the Tender Committee formed an opinion that these three big manufacturers formed a cartel and also quoted an unworkable predatory price at the post-tender stage. therefore from the point of view of preventing monopoly in the public interest the decision in question was then in a bonafide manner. However, on a factual basis we held that the alleged formation of a cartel was only in the realm of suspicion and in that view the decision was modified, as already indicated. However, we make it clear that the said modifications by way of judicial review is not on the ground of legitimate expectation and violative of principles of natural justice but on the other ground namely the decision of the authorities was based on wrong assumption of formation of a cartel.

It may be mentioned that status of a manufacturer being a BIFR company or a small manufacturers was not taken into account so far as the fixation of the price is concerned and these considerations were deemed relevant only for the purpose of allocation of quantities. The stand taken by the Railways is that smaller manufacturers should survive from the point of view of arrest in monopolistic tendencies and from the point of view of public interest. The Tender Committee proceedings would indicate that on the basis of certain formulae namely the past performance, capacity etc. the allotment was being made. therefore these can not be said to be irrelevant considerations and as a matter of fact they had been duly given effect to and weightage was given accordingly in respect of allotment of quantities to various manufacturers within the four corners of the limited tender.

Now coming to the question of dual pricing, the submission is that in respect of same set of manufacturers, some of them can not be made to supply at a lower price and the others namely smaller manufacturers can not be given advantage to supply at a higher price and such dual pricing is unreasonable and arbitrary. As already noted, the Tender Committee worked out an upgraded price and taking into other relevant factors like cost of the material etc. into consideration and applying the formula as was being done in the past and particularly taking into consideration the two concessions in respect of custom and freight fixed Rs. 76,000/- as the reasonable price. This was very close to the price quoted by the three big manufacturers. But at a post-tender stage, they entered into correspondence offering a lower price and ultimately the three big manufacturers committed themselves to supply at the rate of Rs. 67,000/- per bogie. In our earlier order we indicated that these big manufacturers formed a different category namely that they may be in a position to supply at that rate as is evident from their own commitment but to apply the same price which is much lower than the reasonable and workable price fixed by the Tender Committee to other smaller manufacturers would again result in ending the competition between the big and the small which ultimately would result in monopoly of the market by the three big manufacturers. That is a very important consideration from the point of view of public interest. However, as already mentioned we directed the Tender Committee to consider the matter afresh and even if it results in dual pricing, it would not be bad in the circumstances mentioned above.

• • •

CHAPTER XIII

B. Himmatlal Agrawal vs. Competition Commission of India and Ors. (18.05.2018 - SC)

Equivalent Citation:2018(190)AIC200, AIR2018SC2804, AIR2018SC2804, 2018 (3) CCC 66 , 2018(3) CHN (SC) 256, [2018]144CLA275(SC), 2018CompLR507(Supreme Court), III(2018)CPJ1(SC), (2018)190PLR736, 2018(7)SCALE614, 2018 (5) SCJ 564, [2018]148SCL111(SC)

Relevant Section:

Competition act, 2002 - section 53b

Hon'ble Judges/Coram:

A.K. Sikri and Ashok Bhushan, JJ.

Number of pages in the original judgment- 5

Case Note:

Anti-competitive practices - Non-compliance of direction - Dismissal of appeal - Challenge thereto - Section 53(b) of Competition Act, 2002 (Act) - Whether order of National Company Law Appellate Tribunal ('Appellate Tribunal') dismissing main appeal of Appellant for non-compliance of direction to deposit amount as a condition for grant of stay is justified and legal?

Facts

The Appellant herein is a partnership firm, engaged in the business of transportation of coal and sand since 1981. In June, 2014, the Appellant firm participated in two tenders, bearing numbers 03/2014-15 and 06/2014-15 floated by the Respondent No. 2 herein i.e. M/s. Western Coalfields Limited. The Appellant firm was L-II and not the lowest bidder for allotment of the tenders. In June, 2015, the Appellant firm received a notice from the Competition Commission of India, New Delhi (hereinafter referred to as 'CCI') asking to show cause Under Section 19(1)(a) read with Section 3 of the Competition Act, 2002 (hereinafter referred to as the 'Act'). In the said notice, it was alleged that the Appellant firm was involved in anti-competitive and unfair trade practices in collusion with nine other firms. The Appellant firm filed its reply. The CCI after considering the same passed orders Under Section 26 of the Act and directed the inquiry to be conducted by the Director General (DG) of the CCI. DG submitted its report after the inquiry giving his findings to the effect that the Appellant had indulged in anti-competitive and unfair trade practices in collusion with the other firms. The Appellant was given a chance to file its objections thereto. After considering those objections, the CCI passed orders dated September 14, 2017 affirming the findings of the DG and imposed penalties on the Appellant firm as well as nine parties. Insofar as Appellant is concerned, penalty of Rs. 3.61 crores has been imposed.

3. The Appellant filed the statutory appeal there against before the Appellate Tribunal which was registered as Competition Appeal (AT) No. 24/2017. The Appellant also prayed for interim stay of the penalty order. Arguments were heard on admission as well as on stay. Vide orders dated November 20, 2017, Appellate Tribunal admitted the appeal. It also granted stay on the orders of the CCI with the condition of depositing 10% of the total penalty (i.e. a sum of Rs. 36,12,222/-) imposed by CCI, to be paid by the Appellant, within two weeks i.e. by December 4, 2017. The Appellant could not fulfill the said condition of deposit. When the matter was taken up on December 4, 2017, the Appellant pleaded before the Appellate Tribunal that non-compliance because of financial crunch which the Appellant was facing. The Appellate Tribunal, however, passed orders dated December 4, 2017 to the following effect:

By way of last opportunity, the Appellant is given time till 20th December, 2017 to deposit 10% of the penalty amount, failing which, the appeal stands disposed without referring further to the bench.

4. As per the Appellant, since it was in deep financial trouble, it could not deposit the amount by December 20, 2017 in spite of all bona fide intentions. The Appellant accordingly filed I.A. No. 84 of 2017 on December 18, 2017 seeking modification of orders dated December 4, 2017. It was stated in the said application that it had incurred net loss of Rs. 3,72,45,393.94 for the Financial Year 2016-17 and, therefore, was not in a position to deposit the said amount. The request of the Appellant was, however, not acceded to and vide orders dated December 21, 2017, the Appellate Tribunal has dismissed I.A. No. 84 of 2017. At the same time, it has dismissed the appeal of the Appellant as well for non-compliance of its order dated December 4, 2017.

Held while allowing the appeal

Order of CCI was challenged by filing appeal under Section 53B of Act. Along with appeal, Appellant had also filed application for stay of operation of order of CCI during pendency of appeal. Appeal was admitted insofar as stay was concerned, which was granted subject to condition that, Appellant deposited 10 per cent of amount of penalty imposed by CCI. Condition of deposit was attached to order of stay. In case of non-compliance of said condition, consequence would be that stay had ceased to operate as condition for stay was not fulfilled. However, noncompliance of conditional order of stay would have no bearing insofar as main appeal was concerned. Right to appeal was statutorily provided under Section 53B of Act, aforesaid provision, thus, conferred a right upon any of aggrieved parties mentioned therein to prefer an appeal to Appellate Tribunal. This statutory provision did not impose any condition of pre-deposit for entertaining appeal. Therefore, right to file appeal, if it was filed within period of limitation, was conferred by statute and that could not be taken away by imposing condition of deposit of an amount leading to dismissal of main appeal itself, if said condition was not satisfied. Sub-section (3) of Section 53B specifically casted a duty upon Appellate Tribunal to pass order on appeal, as it thought fit i.e. either confirming, modifying or setting aside direction, decision or order appealed against. It was to be done after giving an opportunity of hearing to parties to the appeal. It, thus, clearly implied that, appeal had to be decided on merits. Appellate Tribunal, which was creature of a statute, had to act within domain prescribed by law/statutory provision. This provision nowhere stipulated that, Appellate Tribunal could direct Appellant to deposit a certain amount as a condition precedent for hearing appeal. Condition of deposit of 10 per cent of penalty was imposed insofar as stay of penalty order passed by CCI was concerned. Therefore, at most, stay could have been vacated. Appellate Tribunal, thus, had no jurisdiction to dismiss appeal itself. Accordingly, part of impugned order was set aside and appeal shall be decided by Appellate Tribunal on merits. So far as stay of penalty order was concerned, that stood vacated for non-compliance of condition of deposit of 10 per cent of penalty and, thus, there was no stay of CCI order in favour of Appellant.

• • •

CHAPTER XIV

Competition Commission of India vs. Steel Authority of India Ltd. and Ors. (09.09.2010 - SC)

Relevant Section:

Competition Act, 2002 - Section 3; Uttar Pradesh Imposition of Ceiling on Land Holdings Act, 1960 - Section 12, Uttar Pradesh Imposition of Ceiling on Land Holdings Act, 1960 - Section 13; Competition Act, 2002 - Section 53B

Equivalent Citation: 2010(5)ALLMR(SC)934, 2010 (4) CCC 55 , [2010]98CLA278(SC), 2010CompLR61(SupremeCourt), (2010)4CompLJ1(SC),JT2010(10)SC26,(2011)2MLJ271(SC), 2010(9)SCALE291,(2010)10SCC744, [2010]103SCL269(SC), [2010]11SCR112, 2010(8)UJ4093

Hon'ble Judges/Coram:

S.H. Kapadia, C.J., K.S. Panicker Radhakrishnan and Swatanter Kumar, JJ.

Number of pages in the original judgment- 35

Case Note:

Competition - Invocation of provisions of Competition Act before Competition Commission by Informant - Direction for investigation into matter by Commission on basis of existence of prima facie case - Challenge against thereto before Appellate Tribunal - Section 26(1) and Section 53A(1) of Competition Act, 2002 - Whether the directions passed by the Commission in exercise of its powers under Section 26(1) of the Act forming a prima facie opinion would be appealable in terms of Section 53A(1) of the Act

Facts

8. Jindal Steel & Powers Ltd. (for short the 'informant') invoked the provisions of Section 19 read with Section 26(1) of the Act by providing information to the Commission alleging that M/s. Steel Authority of India Ltd. (for short 'SAIL') had, inter alia, entered into an exclusive supply agreement with Indian Railways for supply of rails. The SAIL, thus, was alleged to have abused its dominant position in the market and deprived others of fair competition and therefore, acted contrary to Section 3(4) (Anti-competitive Agreements) and Section 4(1) (Abuse of dominant position) of the Act. This information was registered by the Commission

and was considered in its meeting held on 27th October, 2008 on which date the matter was deferred at the request of the informant for furnishing additional information. During the course of hearing, it was also brought to the notice of the Commission that a petition being Writ Petition (C) No. 8531 of 2009, filed by the informant against the Ministry of Railways, was also pending in the High Court of Delhi at New Delhi. Vide order dated 10th November, 2009 the Commission directed the informant to file an affidavit with respect to the information furnished by it. The Commission also directed SAIL to submit its comments in respect of the information received by the Commission within two weeks from the date of the said meeting and the matter was adjourned till 8th December, 2009. On 19th November, 2009 a notice was issued to SAIL enclosing all information submitted by the informant. When the matter was taken up for consideration by the Commission on 8th December, 2009, the Commission took on record the affidavit filed by the informant on 30th November, 2009 in terms of the earlier order of the Commission, but SAIL requested extension of six weeks time to file its comments. Finding no justification in the request of the SAIL, the Commission, vide its order dated 8th December, 2009, declined the prayer for extension of time. In this order, it also formed the opinion that prima facie case existed against SAIL, and resultantly, directed the Director General, appointed under Section 16(1) of the Act, to make investigation into the matter in terms of Section 26(1) of the Act. It also granted liberty to SAIL to file its views and comments before the Director General during the course of investigation. Despite these orders, SAIL filed an interim reply before the Commission along with an application that it may be heard before any interim order is passed by the Commission in the proceedings. On 22nd December, 2009 the Commission only reiterated its earlier directions made to the Director General for investigation and granted liberty to SAIL to file its reply before the Director General. The correctness of the directions contained in the order dated 8th December, 2009 was challenged by SAIL before the Competition Appellate Tribunal (for short, the 'Tribunal'). The Commission filed an application on 28th January, 2010 before the Tribunal seeking impleadment in the appeal filed by SAIL. It also filed an application for vacation of interim orders which had been issued by the Tribunal on 11th January, 2010, staying further proceedings before the Director General in furtherance of the directions of the Commission dated 8th December, 2009.

Commission was of the opinion that there exists a prima facie case. Therefore, the Commission decided that the case be referred to Director General for investigation in the matter.

Secretary was accordingly directed to refer the case to DG for investigation and submission of the report within 45 days of the receipt of orders of the Commission. SAIL informed that they may furnish their views/comments in the matter to the DG.

9. As already noticed, the legality of this order was questioned before the Tribunal by SAIL on one hand, while, on the other hand the Commission had pressed its application for impleadment. In the application for impleadment it was averred by the Commission that it is a necessary and proper party for adjudication of the matter before the Tribunal and therefore, it should be impleaded as a party and be heard in accordance with law. Emphasis was also placed on Section 18 of the Act to contend that powers, functions and duties of the Commission were such that it would always be appropriate for the Commission to be impleaded as a party in appeals filed before the Tribunal. It was also averred in the application that intervention of the Commission at the appellate proceedings would not prejudice anybody. The very maintainability of the appeal before the Tribunal was also questioned by the Commission on the ground that the order under appeal before the Tribunal was a direction simpliciter to conduct investigation and thus was not an order appealable within the meaning of Section 53A of the Act. The Tribunal in its order dated 15th February, 2010, inter alia, but significantly held as under:

(a) The application of the Commission for impleadment was dismissed, as in the opinion of the Tribunal the Commission was neither a necessary nor a proper party in the appellate proceedings before the Tribunal. Resultantly, the application for vacation of stay also came to be dismissed.

(b) It was held that giving of reasons is an essential element of administration of justice. A right to reason is, therefore, an indispensable part of sound system of judicial review. Thus, the Commission is directed to give reasons while passing any order, direction or taking any decision.

(c) The appeal against the order dated 8th December, 2009 was held to be maintainable in terms of Section 53A of the Act. While setting aside the said order of the Commission and recording a finding that there was violation of principles of natural justice, the Tribunal granted further time to SAIL to file reply by 22nd February, 2010 in addition to the reply already filed by SAIL.

10. This order of the Tribunal dated 15th February, 2010 is impugned in the present appeal.

Held while partly allowing the appeal

Direction under Section 26(1) after formation of a prima facie opinion is a direction simpliciter to cause an investigation into the matter - Issuance of such a direction, at the face of it, is an administrative direction to one of its own wings departmentally and is without entering upon any adjudicatory process - It does not effectively determine any right or obligation of the parties to the lis and does not entail civil consequences for any person and therefore, is not appealable

Competition - Right of appeal - Section 26(1) and Section 53A(1) of Competition Act, 2002 - Held, Right to appeal, being a statutory right, is controlled strictly by the provision and the procedure prescribing such a right. Therefore, no other direction, decision or order of the Commission is appealable except those expressly stated in Section 53A(1)(a)

Competition - Direction for investigation into matter by Commission on basis of existence of prima facie case - Challenge against thereto on ground of non-issuance of notice - Whether the parties, including the informant or the affected party, are entitled to notice or hearing, as a matter of right, at the preliminary stage of formulating an opinion as to the existence of the prima facie case - Held, the jurisdiction of the Commission, to act under this provision, does not contemplate any adjudicatory function - Commission is not expected to give notice to the parties, i.e. the informant or the affected parties and hear them at length, before forming its opinion - Right of notice of hearing is not contemplated under the provisions of Section 26(1) of the Act - However, Regulation 17(2) gives right to Commission for seeking information

Competition - Impleadment of Competition Commission in Appellate proceedings as necessary or proper party - Section 19 and Section 26 of Competition Act, 2002 - Whether the Commission would be a necessary or a proper party in the proceedings before the Tribunal in an appeal preferred by any party - Held, the Commission, in terms of Section 19 read with Section 26 of the Act, is entitled to commence proceedings suo moto and adopt its own procedure for completion of such proceedings - In cases where proceedings are initiated suo moto by the Commission, the Commission is a necessary party - However, in other cases commission would not only help in expeditious disposal, but the Commission, as an expert body, in any case, is entitled to participate in its proceedings in terms of Regulation 51

Competition - Scope and power of Competition Commission to issue interim orders - Section 33 of Competition Act, 2002 and Regulation 18(2) of the Competition Commission of India (General) Regulations, 2009 - Held, the power under Section 33 of the Act to pass temporary restraint order can only be exercised by the Commission when it has formed prima facie opinion and directed investigation in terms of Section 26(1) of the Act, as is evident from the language of this provision read with Regulation 18(2) of the Regulations - Thus, it has the power to pass ad interim ex parte injunction orders, but only upon recording its due satisfaction as well as its view that the Commission deemed it necessary not to give a notice to the other side

• • •

CHAPTER XV

Delhi Development Authority vs. P.R. Samanta (21.07.2015 - SC

Relevant Section:

Monopolies and restrictive trade practices act, 1969 [repealed] - section 36a

Equivalent Citation: 2015VIII AD (S.C.) 245, 2015(154)AIC236, AIR2015SC3035, AIR2015SC3035, 2015(5)ALLMR907, 2015 (3) CCC 198 , 2016(1)CDR164(SC), [2016]132CLA69(SC), 2015CompLR789(Supreme Court), (2015)4CompLJ336(SC), 2015 (3) CPR 453 , 2015(153)DRJ115, (2015)6MLJ626(SC), 2015(4)RCR(Civil)634, 2015(8)SCALE91, (2015)14SCC501, 2015 (9) SCJ 286, [2016]134SCL500(SC)

Hon'ble Judges/Coram:

Vikramajit Sen and S.K. Singh, JJ.

Number of pages in the original judgment-5

Case Note:

MRTP/Competition Laws - Refund of registration amount - Rate of interest payable - Reasonableness thereof - Appellant refunded registration amount along with interest in terms of offer document - Respondent alleged that interest paid was at rate lower than rate at which Respondent was to be charged in case of default - Commission allowed higher rate of interest - Whether Commission should not have enhanced contract rate of interest on ground that it was less than one charged from Respondent when in default.

Facts:

The Appellant chose to accept the proposal for cancellation of allotment made by the Respondent but it refunded the registration amount along with interest in terms of the offer document which had been accepted by the Respondent and was thus the rate finalized by agreement between the parties.

The Respondent in his complaint before the Commission raised grievance that the interest paid on the registration amount was at a rate lower than the rate at which the Respondent was to be charged in case of delay/default.

The Commission positively considered the Respondent's main grievance against the payment of the interest on the registration amount and awarded a higher rate of interest on the registration amount as against the one paid by the Respondent. Hence, this present appeal.

Held, allowing the appeal:

(1) The Commission has clearly erred in interfering with the contractual rate of interest in absence of any finding against the actions and orders of the Appellant. Without returning a finding that there was any unfair trade practice under the provisions of the Act, the Commission clearly erred in compensating the Respondent with a higher rate of interest. Even the basis for grant of higher interest is without discussion of any material. The order under appeal indicates no material for coming to the impugned finding that payment of interest on the registration amount should not be less than one charged from the applicants when they commit a default. A default clause is introduced to deter any delay or default and hence such penalty is by its very nature a deterrent one. That by itself offers a reasonable justification for the Appellant to charge a higher rate of interest in the case of delay/default. So far as interest on the registration amount is concerned it stands on a different footing. In absence of relevant pleadings and evidence it cannot be presumed that the Appellant has resorted to any unfair trade practice as defined under Section 36A MRTP Act, 1969 or has increased its price unreasonably or made unreasonable earnings by investing the registration amount in accounts bearing higher interest. The relevant provision in the Brochure of the Scheme by itself does not appear to be unreasonable in allowing interest as claimed by the Appellant. Nothing has been brought to notice which may show that the registration amount is to remain locked for any fixed term or that the Appellant can refuse an application for cancellation of registration at an early stage or even before draw of lots for allotment/allocation of flats. In such a situation it is not possible to infer that the registration deposits must reasonably be kept in long term fixed deposits with a view to earn higher interests. In any case such aspects had to be pleaded and proved by the Respondent before the Commission but that has not been done leading to absence of requisite findings. [10]

(2) The impugned order of the Commission awarding interest at the enhanced rate of interest on the registration amount and also awarding litigation charges is against law and unjustified. The impugned judgment and order is therefore set aside. The appeal stands allowed. [11]

• • •

CHAPTER XVI

Peico Electronics and Electricals and Ors. vs. Union of India (UOI) and Ors. (09.03.2004 - SC)

Relevant Section:

Monopolies And Restrictive Trade Practices Act, 1969 [repealed] - Section 33

Equivalent Citation:2004(17)AIC921, [2004]59CLA276(SC), (2004)2CompLJ193(SC),(2004)2CompLJ193(SC), II(2004)CPJ3(SC), 2004 (2) CPR 52 , (2004)3MLJ159(SC), 2004(3)SCALE175, (2004)3SCC658, [2004]51SCL132(SC), [2004]2SCR883

Hon'ble Judges/Coram:

P. Venkatarama Reddi and S.H. Kapadia, JJ.

Number of pages in the original judgment- 9

Case Note:

MRTP - Monopolies and Restrictive Trade Practices Act, 1969 - Sections 33(1), 55 - Appellant company engaged in manufacture and sale of audio products, entered into agreement with R2, appointing him as its dealer - Termination of dealership agreement by appellant company - Complaint filed by R2 before commission - Commission holding that appellant indulged in certain restrictive trade practices, directed appellant to desist from indulging in such practices and to amend offending clause in dealership agreement and not to give effect to termination of dealership of complainant and to ensure supply of Philips products to extent of supply made in year 1985 - Appeal - Since finding on record to show that appellant imposed restriction on complainant from selling products from Sarafa Bazar shop of complainant, act of appellant fell within ambit of Section 33(1)(g) - Since no finding with respects of crucial ingredients of Section 2(o)(ii), findings of discrimination to other dealer held to be not proved - The Commission was held to be justified in holding that Clause 7 of the Agreement was a restrictive trade practice within the meaning of Clause (g) of Section 33(1) of M.R.T.P. Act and it had effect of distorting or restricting competition - Commission exceeded its jurisdiction in giving a direction not to give effect to the letter terminating the Agreement and to restore the supplies to the complainant - The 'cease and desist' order passed under Section 37(1)(a) held otiose and inoperative in view of fact that the contract stood terminated

Facts

The appellant Company manufactures and sells certain audio products. It has a vast network of dealers--about 1800 throughout the country who are appointed on principal to principal basis. In Gwalior, the appellant had a dealer by name M/s. Evergreen operating since long from its shop at Sarafa Bazar. In the year 1985, the appellant appointed the 2nd respondent (hereinafter referred to as 'R-2' or 'complainant') having its place of business at Gwalior as another dealer. An agreement dated 15.11.1985 which, it is not in dispute, is in standard form was entered into. Clause 29 of the Agreement provided for termination of agreement by either party by giving to the other 30 days notice in writing. In terms of this clause, the appellant by its notice dated 23.9.1987 gave 30 days notice to R-2, terminated the dealership on expiry of the notice period. According to the appellant, such a step was taken as it was not satisfied with the performance of R-2. R-2 then filed a complaint before the Commission. The complainant alleged that the appellant felt aggrieved by some of the letters addressed by the complainant pointing out preferential treatment to the old dealer M/s. Evergreen to the detriment of R-2. Certain instances of restrictive trade practices were enumerated in the complaint. The complainant prayed for the issuance of 'cease and desist order' and a direction to restore the dealership and resume supplies of Philips products. The Commission decided to hold an enquiry. Accordingly, a notice of enquiry was sent to the appellant on 21.1.1988. In the said notice, as many as five restrictive trade practices alleged to have been committed by the appellant were set out. They are as follows:

(i) The respondents prohibited the complainant from dealing in or selling the same type of products of the competitors. The practice is restrictive trade practice within the meaning of Section 33(1)(c) of the MRTP Act;

(ii) The respondents supplied to the complainant all types of goods irrespective of its order. For instance supply of 252 pcs of infra lamps was made to the complainant on 31st December, 1985 even though the complainant had not placed any order for them. Thus the respondent in a trade practice of full line forcing/ dumping unwanted goods and also delaying with holding the supply of wanted and ordered goods. It is a restrictive trade practice within the meaning of Section 2(o) and Section 33(1)(b) of the Act. The practice is a restrictive trade practice within the meaning of Section 33(1)(b) of the MRTP Act.

(iii) The complainant was allocated a particular territory to which its dealership was confined. The practice of allocating a territory is a restrictive trade practice within the meaning of Section 33(1)(g) of the MRTP Act.

(iv) The respondent fixed the prices at which their products were to be sold without giving liberty to the complainant to sell at prices lower to its customers. The practice is a restrictive trade practice within the meaning of Section 33(1)(f) of the MRTP Act.

(v) The respondent discriminated against the complainant and gave a favoured treatment to their other dealer, viz. Evergreen, Sarafa Bazar, Gwalior in making supplies of Philip products. The practice is a restrictive trade practice within the meaning of Section 2(o)(ii) of the MRTP Act.

3. It appears that during the pendency of the inquiry, the Commission issued an order of ad interim injunction, However, it was stayed by the Bombay High Court on a writ petition filed by the appellant.

Held while disposing off the appeal

As per the charge, the appellant gave a favourable treatment to the other dealer, namely, M/s Evergreen in making supplies of Philips products and thus the appellant discriminated against the complainant. In the context of this allegation, the real grievance made out by the complainant is that fast moving and popular products were being supplied to M/s Evergreen, whereas the complainant was mostly getting slow moving items. It was further alleged that M/s Evergreen was free to sell the Philips products from their showroom at Sarafa Bazar to any non Philips products dealers not only at Gwalior but also in four other Districts whereas the same facility was denied to the complainant. The charge of discrimination was held established only on the ground that M/s Evergreen was given freedom to sell the appellant's products from Sarafa Bazaar, but the complainant was not allowed to sell from its Sarafa Bazaar shop. This, according to the Commission, has resulted in discriminatory treatment against the complainant, attracting Section 2(o)(ii) of the Act.

There is no finding whatsoever with respect to one of the crucial ingredients of Section 2(o)(ii). Moreover, we find nothing in the evidence to enable the Commission to arrive at a finding on the question whether the set of the appellant in disallowing the complainant from effecting the sales from its second shop at Sarafa Bazaar had resulted in or likely to result in the imposition of unjustified burden on the consumers. We are therefore of the view that the Commission's finding under charge No. (v) that the appellant resorted to restrictive trade practice within the meaning of Section 2(o)(ii) is legally erroneous and is liable to be set aside.

The Commission can suo motu enquire into such trade practices and take necessary follow-up action. The knowledge or information can as well be derived from the facts disclosed in the complaint petition, the pleadings or from the material adduced in the case. The Commission will be failing in its duty if it does not take note of restrictive trade practices that come to its notice in the course of enquiry into a complaint. In our considered view, the omission to record a formal proceeding framing an issue or the point for suo motu consideration does not by itself vitiate the decision of the Commission. However, it is implicit in the exercise of such power that adequate opportunity ought to be given to the affected party to meet the point which is the subject matter of suo motu enquiry. There is no bar to the combination of an enquiry into the allegations made by the complainant and the suo motu enquiry into a matter coming to its notice, in testing the validity of the action taken by the Commission from the procedural angle, the approach of the Court should be such as to promote the objectives of the Act. A narrow or pedantic approach ought to be eschewed. Viewed from this angle, we are unable to hold that the Commission out-stepped its limits in testing the legality of Clause 7 or that the appellant was handicapped in meeting its case on account of non framing of 'charge' relating to Clause 7 of the Agreement.

The next question is whether in view of termination of Agreement, the Commission was precluded from probing into the validity of the relevant clause in the Agreement. It is not in dispute that the clause of this nature is incorporated in all the Agreements entered into with the dealers. In other words, the Agreement is in a standard form. As held by the Commission, apart from the fact that Clause 7 per se is a restrictive trade practice, it has the potential of giving rise to restrictive trade practices in future. Therefore, the Commission, in exercise of its power under Clause (b) of Section 37(1), directed that the clause should be suitably amended so as to remove the offensive sting in it. Having regard, to our decision on Contention No. 3, the Commission's directive cannot be implemented in so far as the present Agreement is concerned. At the same time, the appellant shall not be allowed to perpetuate the unfair trade practice inherent in Clause 7 of the standard form Agreement. We, therefore; consider it just and proper to modify the order of Commission by directing that the appellant should take steps to purge the restrictive trade practice by suitably amending Clause 7 or identical clause wherever it occurs in all the Agreements with its dealers and file a report to the Commission accordingly.

The conclusions we have reached are summed up as follows:

1. The finding of the Tribunal on charge No. iii is upheld.

2. The Finding in respect of the charge No. v is unsustainable.

3. The Commission is justified in holding that Clause 7 of the Agreement is a restrictive trade practice within the meaning of Clause (g) of Section 33(1) of M.R.T.P. Act and it has the effect of distorting or restricting competition. The direction of the Commission to amend Clause 7 suitably is correct. Irrespective of the termination of the Agreement between appellant and R-2, the appellant should take steps to amend a similar clause existing in other agreements of similar nature with the dealers.

4. The Commission exceeded its jurisdiction in giving a direction not to give effect to the letter terminating the Agreement and to restore the supplies to the complainant. Such a direction cannot be sustained in the absence of a finding that the termination of Agreement was contrary to the provisions of the Act or it is a device to circumvent the provisions of the Act so as to perpetuate the restrictive trade practice.

5. The 'cease and desist' order passed under Section 37(1)(a) becomes otiose and inoperative in view of the fact that the contract stands terminated. The remedy of the complainant (R-2) is to pursue his claim for compensation under Section 12B for the loss suffered by him on account of the restrictive trade practice covered by charge No. iii.

• • •

CHAPTER XVII

Raymond Woollen Mills Ltd. and Ors. vs. Director General (Investigation and Registration) and Ors. (15.05.2008 - SC)

Relevant Section:

Monopolies and restrictive trade practices act, 1969 [repealed] - section 38(1)(h)

Equivalent Citation:AIR2009SC399, 2008 (2) CCC 344 , [2008]85CLA1(SC), 2008-4-LW803, 2008(8)SCALE586, (2008)12SCC73, [2008]84SCL309(SC)

Hon'ble Judges/Coram:

Tarun Chatterjee and Dalveer Bhandari, JJ.

Number of pages in the original judgment - 9

Facts

1. Brief facts which are necessary to dispose of this appeal are as under:

A Notice of Enquiry under Section 10(a)(iv) and Section 37 of the Monopolies and Restrictive Trade Practices Act, 1969 (hereinafter referred to as the `MRTP Act') was issued to the appellants wherein it was alleged that the appellants had indulged in restrictive trade practice within the meaning of Section 2(o)(ii) and Section 33(1)(b) and of the MRTP Act.

4. The appellants herein denied the allegations made in the Notice of Enquiry and it was categorically stated that it neither manufactured nor sold any garments and such allegations of restrictive trade practice made against it was without any foundation.

The Commission, after evaluating the evidence, observed that 133 trousers were supplied to the complainant/informant in the year 1985-86. However, no record of the order placed with the appellants could be produced, but the complainant/informant stated that he was compelled by the appellants to place substantial order for trousers in order to get supplies of blazers, safaris and suits. The invoices which were produced as part of evidence revealed the quantity of garments supplied by the appellants and undoubtedly, the quantity of trousers was substantial. It was further observed that there was pressure on the dealers to accept higher quantity of trousers than required and when he showed his unwillingness to accept the large quantity of trousers, his dealership was terminated and the security deposit was refunded to him. The Commission arrived at the conclusion that the allegation of tie-up of sales of trousers with other garments supplied by appellant No. 2 appeared to have been fully established.

12. On the basis of the aforementioned complaint, the Commission arrived at the conclusion that the appellants had indulged in restrictive trade practice within the meaning of Sections 2(o)(ii) and 33(1)(b) of the MRTP Act.

13. The Commission further observed that the termination of the dealership or appellants' refusal to deal with a well established retailer was bound to have an adverse effect and impact on competition in so far as it would reduce the number of retail dealers in the local market and thus would have the effect of restricting and lessening of the competition in the sale and supply of readymade garments and, therefore, would also be prejudicial to public interest. It was further observed that by restricting and reducing the supply of ready to wear garments would also attract the provisions of Section 2(o)(ii) of the MRTP Act.

14. The Commission directed the appellants to cease the aforementioned restrictive trade practice forthwith and furnish an undertaking that they shall not repeat or indulge in same or similar trade practices in future. The Commission further directed the appellants to file an affidavit of compliance within six weeks of the pronouncement of the order.

Held while allowing the appeal

44. The court would be justified in passing the order on alleged restrictive trade practice only when it is "prejudicial to public interest" under Clause (h) of Section 38(1) of the MRTP Act. The pre-condition for passing such an order is that the restriction as imposed directly or indirectly when restricts or discourages competition to any "material degree" in any trade or industry, then only it would be considered as "prejudicial to public interest". The court should not pass an order of "cease and desist" where the alleged restrictive trade practice does not have the impact on restricting competition to any material degree.

45. When the evidence on behalf of the appellants clearly shows that there are several manufacturers including small scale manufactures, the little share of the complainant/informant does not affect the competition in the relevant trade or industry and, accordingly, in these circumstances, to

pass any order under Section 38(1)(h) cannot be justified.

46. In the instant case, the complainant/informant had requested for refund of the security amount and, therefore, it was refunded. It was really not a case of "termination of dealership". There was no charge or allegation of termination of dealership in the notice of enquiry, therefore, the Commission was not justified in passing the order based on "termination of dealership". Even otherwise also, the termination of single dealership cannot affect competition to any "material degree" in the relevant trade or industry within the meaning of Clause (h) of Section 38(1) of the MRTP Act.

• • •

CHAPTER XVIII

Nirma Industries Ltd. vs. Director General of Investigation and Registration (06.05.1997 - SC)

Relevant Section:

Monopolies and restrictive trade practices act, 1969 [repealed] - section 36a

Equivalent Citation:AIR1997SC2382, 1997 (2) CCC 211 , [1997]89CompCas537(SC), (1997)4CompLJ165(SC), II(1997)CPJ10(SC), 1998 (1) CPR 14 , JT1997(5)SC481, 1997(4)SCALE114, (1997)5SCC279, [1997]Supp1SCR137, [1997]95TAXMAN619(SC), 1997(2)UJ191

Hon'ble Judges/Coram:

J.S. Verma, C.J.I. and S.P. Kurdukar, J.

Number of pages in the original judgment - 7

Case Note:

MRTP - sale - Section 36 of Monopolies and Restrictive Trade Practices Act, 1969 - whether company had indulged in any unfair trade practice as provided under Section 36A of Act - whether Order passed against company under Section 36 A (3) (a) is sustainable - having regard to facts and circumstances of case inference of per se presumption against company under Section 36 A (3) (a) of Act unsustainable - company needs to be given opportunity to prove its case that they have not committed any unfair trade practice under Act and finding is necessary in order to determine whether such unfair trade practice had caused loss or injury to consumers of such goods by eliminating or restricting competition or otherwise.

Facts

2. Briefly stated the facts of the case are as under :

The appellant a public limited company (for short 'the company) having its registered office at Ahmedabad, is engaged in manufacture and sale of Nirma washing powder, Nirma detergent cakes and Nirma bath soaps. The company has been manufacturing these products since early seventies and its products are marketed and sold all over the country. It is the claim of the appellant that having established a good market for sale of its various products and having captured the confidence of the consumers, thought of offering a scheme as an incentive to the consumers for its products. The appellant, therefore, on April 25, 1991, floated a scheme of awarding and distributing of prizes through a lottery. According to the scheme, the appellant placed a coupon bearing a number in each one kg. pack of detergent/washing powder. The said scheme was valid till July 31, 1991 and the draw of lots was to be held on August 30, 1991. The coupon kept in the one kg. bag of detergent mentioned that prizes worth Rs. 71 lacs were to be distributed which included Contessa Car, Maruti 800 Car, BPL TV set, golden chain, Titan watch, Steel jug, Ladies purse, Steel bawl set and cash.

3. On July 24, 1991, a complaint was received by the D.G. (I & R) from Azad Singh, New Delhi, alleging, inter alia, that the company while floating a scheme in question did not inform the customer as to in which newspaper the result would be published; the company had increased the price of the detergent along with prize scheme; the said scheme is harming the interest of the other companies in this competition and the condition of the coupon is so bad that while opening the bag, it would get torn and the winner of the prize will have to face difficulty in getting the prize which would help the company in evading the responsibility to give the prize. Azad Singh, therefore, prayed that action be taken against the company and "save the poor people being robbed." The D.G. very promptly responded to the complaint of Azad Singh and filed an application on July 26, 1991 before the Commission for investigation and registration of the complaint under Section 36B(c) of the Act. The D.G. requested the Commission hold an inquiry into the unfair trade practices under Section 36D(1) of the Act and pass an order of cease and desist against the company. It was alleged in the complaint that the scheme in question floated by the Company was with a view to promote the sale of its detergent powder; that it lured the customers to purchase more and more Nirma detergent powder under the temptation of getting the prizes; that this trade practice of offering prizes would lead to excessive purchases and consumption by the customers in the expectation of getting prizes; that such avoidable and the excessive purchases were real loss to the consumers and that it had deleterious impact on competition inasmuch as extraneous consideration other than quality and the price of the product tend to determine the consumer preference; that there are several detergent manufacturers in India; that the impugned scheme of the respondent affected, distorted and restricted competition among the various manufacturers of detergent powder and that the conduct of lottery or game of chance for the purpose of promoting the sale, use or supply of detergent powder by the appellant amounted to an unfair trade practice within the meaning of Section 36A(3)(a) and (b) of the Act. It

was then alleged by the D.G. in his complaint that company had increased the price of its detergent powder just prior to the launching of the scheme with an intention to recover the value of the prizes fully or partly from the consumers by raising the prices of its products. The company, therefore, had indulged in unfair trade practice under Section 36A(3)(a) and (b) of the Act. The D.G., therefore, recommended that the Commission would inquire into the complaint and pass cease and desist order against the company.

1. The Commission on the basis of the above pleadings formulated four issues for its consideration and heard the Advocates for the parties. The Commission vide its impugned order found that the company has not committed the breach of Section 36A(3)(b) of the Act and the charge in that behalf is unsustainable. The Commission, however, found that the charge against the company under Section 36A(3)(a) of the Act is proved and accordingly directed the company not to repeat the same in future. It is this order of the Commission dated January 4, 1996 which is subject matter of challenge in this appeal.

Section 36C provides investigation by Director General before an issue of process in certain cases. In the present case, the Director General on receipt of the complaint on July 24, 1991 from one Shri Azad Singh, perused the same and immediately on July 26, 1991 submitted his application to the Commission for making inquiry and for suitable action under Section 36D of the Act.

Held while disposing off the appeal

14. The Commission in its impugned order held that the gift/prize scheme floated by the company amounted to unfair trade practices under Section 36A(3)(a) of the Act and to support this finding, the only material placed before the Commission was the complaint filed by the D.G. containing an averment that the company had raised the prices of its detergent a few days before the impugned scheme was floated. The finding of the Commission in this behalf proceeds on the footing that the prize money under the impugned scheme was either fully or partly covered by the amount charged in the transaction as a whole. Should this averment in the complaint of the D.G. be presumed to be per se valid being a proof of an unfair trade practice under Section 36A(3)(a) of the Act? The Commission appears t& have been influenced by its own unreported decisions wherein

such a view was taken and followed. Mr. Dushyant, Learned Senior Advocate for the appellant urged that the Commission had not taken into account the reply filed on behalf of the company that the prices of the detergent powder were required to be raised because of rise in the prices of the raw materials. If the Commission were to call upon the company to justify the increase in the prices of the detergent powder dehors the prize money-the Company would have produced the material to dislodge the assumption that this increase in the prices of the detergent powder was not bonafide and in fact an exercise to cover fully or partly the prize money. The learned counsel for the appellant stated before us that the audited balance sheets and other evidence is in their procession which would indicate that the increase in the prices of the detergent powder was necessitated because of increase in the prices of raw materials and other connected factors therewith. For want of sufficient opportunity and under the misconception of law, the company could not produce the evidence on record and, therefore, prayed that the matter be remitted back to the Commission with liberty to the company to produce the relevant evidence on record to substantiate its contentions. Having regard to the facts and circumstances of the case and having come to the conclusion that the inference of per se presumption against the company under Section 36A(3)(a) of the Act was unsustainable. Along with this appeal, the company had produced on record certain documents to justify the increase in the prices of the detergent powder and also sought to prove that the increase in the prices of the detergent powder has no nexus with the prize money covered by the impugned scheme either fully or partly. However, without expressing any opinion in this behalf and to do the justice between the parties, we are of the opinion that the company needs to be given an opportunity to prove its case that they have not committed any unfair trade practice under Section 36A(3)(a) of the Act. Such a finding is necessary in order to determine whether such an unfair trade practice had caused loss or injury to the consumers of such goods by eliminating or restricting competition or otherwise. As stated earlier, except the complaint of the D.G., there was no other material before the Commission which would justify the finding in this behalf. Such an exercise is necessary since any order passed under Section 36D attracts the penal consequences.

15. For the aforesaid conclusions, we are of the opinion that the impugned order of the Commission passed under Section 36D of the Act holding that the company had committed unfair trade practice under

Section 36A(3)(a) of the Act is unsustainable and it is accordingly quashed and set aside. The matter is remitted back to the Commission for disposal afresh in accordance with law after giving an opportunity to both the parties to lead such evidence as they deem fit.

• • •

CHAPTER XIX

G.D.A. and Ors. vs. Mithilesh Goel (26.04.2017 - SC)

Relevant Section:

Monopolies and restrictive trade practices act, 1969 [repealed] - section 36a

Equivalent Citation: AIR2017SC2513, 2017(6)ALLMR439, IV(2017)CPJ45(SC), (2017)14SCC300

Hon'ble Judges/Coram:

Rohinton Fali Nariman and Abhay Manohar Sapre, JJ.

Number of pages in the original judgment - 5

Case Note:

MRTP/Competition Laws - Unfair trade practice - Sections 36A and 36A(1)(ii) of Monopolies and Restrictive Trade Practices Act, 1969 - Complaint made by Respondent who had made application to Appellant-Development Authority for allotment of house - Authority issued allotment letter-cum-payment schedule allotting House to complainant and estimated cost was intimated - Respondent paid sum which was beyond estimated cost - However, Authority intimated final cost of house and demanded balance amount - When complainant protested, Authority kept on upping its demand until finally complainant was constrained to move Commission on ground that upping of this demand in arbitrary fashion would amount to an unfair trade practice - Hence, present appeal - Whether alleged arbitrary up-ping of amount to be paid towards house could possibly be said to be false representation constitute unfair trade practice.

Facts:

A complaint made by Respondent, who had made an application to the Development Authority for allotment of a house. The Authority issued an allotment letter-cum-payment schedule to the complainant and the estimated cost was intimated. However, after seven years, the Authority intimated the final cost of the house and demanded the balance amount. When the complainant protested, the Authority kept on upping its demand until finally the complainant was constrained to move the Monopolies and Restrictive Trade Practices Commission on the ground that the upping of this demand in an arbitrary fashion would amount to an unfair trade practice.

Held, while allowing the appeal:

(i) The unfair trade practice would fall under Section 36A of Act only when goods or the provision of any services are involved. In particular, the unfair trade practice alleged and found in favour of the complainant was under Sub-clause (ii) of Sub-section (1) under which a person falsely represents that the services were of a particular standard, quality or grade. [4]

(ii) The alleged arbitrary up-ping of the amount to be paid towards the house, which was an immovable property, could not possibly be said to be a false representation by the Development Authority that services were of a particular standard, quality or grade. This was for two reasons. First and the foremost, there was no false representation by the Authority, inasmuch as what was communicated to the complainant was only an estimated cost of the house in question. That estimate was revised later owing to several factors. This itself would show that there was no false representation within Section 36A(1)(ii) of the Act. Secondly, what was given was allotment of a house which was an immovable property, and not services of any kind. This being the case, the impugned order must be set aside as it was outside the jurisdiction of the Commission. Accordingly, the impugned judgment passed by the Commission was set aside. [5]

• • •

CHAPTER XX

Haridas Exports vs. All India Float Glass Mfrs. Association and Ors. (22.07.2002 - SC)

Relevant Section:

Monopolies And Restrictive Trade Practices Act, 1969 [repealed]

Equivalent Citation: AIR2002SC2728, [2002]49CLA307(SC), [2002]111CompCas617(SC), (2002)3CompLJ417(SC), II(2002)CPJ11(SC), 2(2002)CPJ11(SC), 2002 (3) CPR 110 , 99(2002)DLT76(SC), 2002(82)ECC683, 2002(105)ECR14(SC), 2002(145)ELT241(S.C.), JT2002(5)SC253, 2002(5)SCALE253, (2002)6SCC600, [2002]38SCL1020(SC), [2002]SUPP1SCR229

Hon'ble Judges/Coram:

B.N. Kirpal, C.J., Y.K. Sabharwal and K.G. Balakrishnan, JJ.

Number of pages inthe original judgment- 23

Case Note:

Held: Jurisdiction - MRTP Act--The MRTP Act does not have extraterritorial operation as the geographical boundaries of its jurisdiction are clearly defined and are limited to India. Thus the MRTP Commission has jurisdiction only over those restrictive trade practices which take place in India.

2. Jurisdiction--MRTP Act--Effects Doctrine--Applicability--Any agreement (even if entered into outside India) that results in a restrictive trade practice in India will fall under the jurisdiction of the MRTP Commission in view of the provisions of Ss. 12A and 37 of the MRTP Act.

3. Jurisdiction--MRTP Commission--Anti-dumping provisions under S. 9A of Customs Tariff Act (CTA) do not imply repeal of S. 33(1)(j) of the MRTP Act, nor do they oust the jurisdiction of the MRTP Commission, since the CTA and the MRTP Act operate in different fields. However, the MRTP Commission has no jurisdiction over matters relating to Import Policy or rates of duty.

4. Temporary Injunction--Cannot be issued under MRTP Act unless conditions laid down under S. 12A(1) ibid are fulfilled. Mere inability of Indian manufacturers to complete with imported goods is no reason to issue a temporary injunction against imports. It has to be proved that the imports involve a restrictive trade practice.

Facts

4. On 10th September, 1998, the respondent No. 1 filed a complainant before the MRTP Commission under Section 33(1)(j), (ja) and Section 36A read with Section 2(o) of the Monopolies and Restrictive Trade Practices Act, 1969 (hereinafter referred to as the 'MRTP Act') against three Indonesian companies alleging that they were manufacturing float glass and were selling the same at predatory prices in India, and were hence resorting to restrictive and unfair trade practices. In the complaint, it was stated that the float glass of Indonesian origin was being exported into India at the CIF price of US$ 155 to 180 PMT. At this price, some float glass had been shipped into India during the period December, 1997 to June, 1998. It was alleged that these sale prices were predatory prices as they were less than not only the cost of production for the product in Indonesia but also the variable cost of production of the product. The complainant gave figures indicating the estimated cost of float glass internationally as well as the cost of production of float glass in India with a view to demonstrate that the Indian manufacturers of float glass would not be able to compete with the price at which the Indonesian manufacturers were presently selling or intending to sell to Indian consumers. On this basis, it was contended that the sale of float glass by the Indonesian manufacturers at the said price of US$ 155 to 180 PMT will restrict, distort and prevent competition by pricing out Indian producers from the market. This would result in lowering the production of the Indian industry and the consequent idle capacity and losses would force the industry to become sick which would lead to its closure which would have a direct impact on the employment in the industry.

5. In response to the notice issued to the Indonesian companies, M/s P.T. Mulia Industries (respondent No. 2 in this appeal) wrote a letter to the MRTP Commission stating that it had never in the past exported float glass to India. The other two respondents did not send any reply to the Commission. The appellant, however, which is the Indian importer of the float glass from Indonesia had filed a caveat before the Commission. It also filed a reply refuting the allegations of the respondent and it was the contention of the appellant that respondent No. 1 was a cartel of Indian manufacturers of float glass which was, in fact, exporting out of India at prices for lower than their own cost of production in India. It was also contended by the appellant herein that the cost of production of float glass was lower in Indonesia than in India and float glass was not being exported

to India at predatory prices.

6. The application under Section 12A for interim injunction was heard by the Chairman of the Commission and a second Member. There was a difference of opinion amongst them. While the Chairman vide order dated 18th January, 1999, allowed the application and restrained the Indonesian companies from exporting to India their float glass production at predatory prices, Dr. S. Chakravarthy, the second Member dismissed the application,inter alia, holding that there was no evidence to substantiate the plea of predatory pricing at this stage. By order dated 9th February, 2000, the third Member who heard the case concurred with the view taken by the Chairman and passed an order of injunction against the Indonesian companies.

Held While allowing the appeal

72. It is in this context that when we examine the provisions of Section 12A, we find that the power of the Commission to grant temporary injunction arises only after it is satisfied that a restrictive trade practice or unfair trade practice is being carried on which is likely to affect prejudicially the public interest or the interest of trader or class of traders etc. It is only with a view to prevent the causing of a prejudicial effect that an interim order can be passed by the Commission under Section 12A.

73. As we have already seen the Act does not have any extra territorial operation. An agreement which is referred to under Section 33(1)(d) must, therefore, be of a kind in which a person in India is a party. This is clear from the bare reading of Explanation I to Section 35. This means that for an agreement to fall within the ambit of Section 33(1)(d) and in respect of which the Commission can exercise its powers under Section 37 a person in India must be regarded as one of the sellers who is a person to such an agreement. This is clear from the use of the words "any party to the agreement carries on business in India" occurring in Explanation I to Section 35. A Careful reading of Section 33(1)(d) indicates that it refers to two classes of agreements. One class is an agreement to purchase goods or to tender for the purchase of goods on list prices or on terms or conditions agreed upon between the purchasers. The other class is an agreement to sell goods or to tender for the sale of goods only at prices or on terms or conditions agreed upon between the sellers. In other words, Section 33(1)(d) refers to the agreements which have the effect of forming either a buyers cartel or a sellers cartel. This sub-section does not refer to or deal with agreements of sale and purchase between sellers and purchasers.

74. In the case of impart of soda ash, the contention is that the appellant is a cartel in America which was proposing to sell soda ash to India at very low prices with a view to eliminate competition and to adversely affect the Indian industry. Any agreement of sale by the appellant to an Indian purchaser would not attract the provisions of Section 33(1)(d), which refers only to cauterizing agreements and not to agreements of sale and purchase. But the MRTP Commission will have jurisdiction under Section 37 to pass orders if such a sale was to amount to being a restrictive trade practice. For the Commission to have jurisdiction to pass such an order whether interim or final, it must come to the conclusion that it is in public interest to do so. It is so borne in mind that public interest does not necessarily mean interest only of the industry. Unless and until it can be demonstrated that an efficient Indian industry would be forced to shut down or suffer serious loss resulting in closure or unemployment, the Commission ought not to pass an injunction restraining an Indian party from importing goods from a cartel at predatory prices. Importing goods at a price lower than what is available in India is not per se illegal. We have provisions under the Customs Act which enables the Government to impose anti-dumping duties with a view to protect the Indian industry. Nevertheless, the era of protectionism is now coming to an end. The Indian industry has to gear up so as to meet the challenges from abroad. If the cartel is selling goods to India and still making profit then it will not be in the interest of the general body of the consumers in India to prevent the import of such goods. The remedy of the Indian industry, in such an event, is to take recourse to the provisions under the Customs Act in relation to the levy of anti-dumping duties.

75. A cartel is formed, inter alia, with a view that members of the cartel do not wage a price war and they sell at an agreed or uniform price. There may perhaps also be a cartel where members divide the territories to which each of them can export. There is little doubt that the object of an export cartel is to capture a market even if at first, it may result in a loss to the exporter.

76. The competition law in the form of MRTP as it stands today does not contain any provision, which can give it jurisdiction to interfere merely with cartel formation. Formation of cartel which takes place outside India is outside the territorial jurisdiction of the MRTP. The Indian importer obtaining goods at a low price does not contravene any law. He has obtained a good bargain.

77. We need not go into the question whether anti-dumping provisions in the Customs Act can be an effective remedy against such cauterization. But if the cartel carries out Restrictive Trade Practice in India or it's actions have the effect of a Restrictive Trade Practice being carried out in India, then the MRTP Commission will get jurisdiction to act under Section 37(1) of the MRTP Act.

78. We make it clear that we are expressing no opinion as to whether the appellant is a cartel or on the question of predatory prices for the reason that we are satisfied that here no case had been made out by the respondents for the grant of injunction against the appellant. The injunction issued against the appellant was not only against the provisions of Section 14 of the Act but even on facts as alleged no case had really beer made out for any order under Section 12A or Section 37 of the Act more so when no import of soda ash into India from the appellant had, in fact, taken place. On the other hand, prima facie the allegation of the appellant that it is the respondents which have formed a cartel and do not welcome any competition does merit consideration, perhaps in another case

• • •

Videos & Tv Shows On Law & Exim

List of some important videos & TV shows on Law & EXIM by Adv. Jayprakash Somani on his YouTube Channel 'Jayprakash Somani EXIM & Legal'

Legal Videos: Hindi -English

1) SLP in Supreme Court / Special Leave Petitions in the Supreme Court of India

2) Transfer of Civil & Criminal Cases by the Supreme Court of India / Transfer of Matrimonial Cases

3) Appellate Jurisdiction of the Supreme Court of India

4) Jurisdictions of the Supreme Court of India

5) Public Interest Litigation in the Supreme Court of India / PIL in Supreme Court

6) Article 32 Writ Petitions in the Supreme Court of India

7) Bail Matters Top 10 Supreme Court Cases

8) FIR Quashing in High Court & Supreme Court

9) Bail & Anticipatory Bail Matters in Supreme Court

10) Insolvency & Bankruptcy Matters in the Supreme Court

11) Insolvency & Bankruptcy Code 2016 Part 1

12) Insolvency & Bankruptcy Code 2016 Part 2

13) Insolvency & Bankruptcy Code 2016 Part 3

14) Corporate Liquidation Process

15) Supreme Court Rules & Procedures Webinar of 2.5 hour on Zoom

16) RDDBFI Act, 1993 (Introduction)

17) The Indian Contact Act 1872

18) Negotiable Instruments Act (Introduction)

19) How to avoid matrimonial disputes& some more videos

20)SEBI Matters in the Supreme Court

21) Matrimonial Matters: Supreme Court's 20 Case Laws

22) Consumer Matters Supreme Court's 20 Case Laws

23) Service Matters Supreme Court's 20 Case Laws

24) How to Search Lawyer for Your Matter

25) Property Matters Supreme Court's 20 Case Laws

26) Bail Matters: Supreme Court's 20 Case Laws

27) Supreme Court / High Court Vacation Benches

28)69000 Teacher's Recruitment Matters of UP Government in the Supreme Court

29) Contempt of Court Matters in the Supreme Court

30) Advocate Act's Matters in the Supreme Court

31) Business Law Matters in the Supreme Court

32) Banking Matters in the Supreme Court

33) Labour Law Matters in the Supreme Court

34) Arbitration Matters in the Supreme Court

35) Careers in Law -Zoom Webinar by Adv. Jayprakash Somani

36) Civil Matters in the Supreme Court

37) Consumer Protection Act | Consumer Matters in the Supreme Court

38) Corporate Matters in the Supreme Court

39) Criminal Matters in the Supreme Court

40) Role of Respondent in the Supreme Court of India

41) Motor Vehicle Accident Matters in Supreme Court with case laws

42) Article 131 Original Suits in Supreme Court

43)PIL in Supreme Court/ Public Interest Litigations in the Supreme Court of India'

44)CAB Citizenship Amendment Bill is not Unconstitutional

45) Supreme Court of India Cases & Process – Marathi

46) Legal Services Export / Export of Legal Services

47) Transfer of Matrimonial Cases by the Supreme Court of India

48) Public Interest Litigation PIL

49) The Specific Relief Act (Introduction)

50) Corporate Insolvency Resolution Process CIRP

51)ABMM's Career 5 - Careers in Law

52) Transfer of cases by Supreme Court

53) Writ Petitions in High Court & Supreme Court of India

54) Supreme Court Jurisdictions - Appeals, SLP, Writ Petitions, Transfer, Original, Review, Curative

55)LEGAL INDIA TV Show: Cases Handled in Supreme Court

56) Corporate Liquidation Process

57) Legal Services Export / Export of Legal Services

• • •

EXIM Videos: Hindi -English

1) Yes, I can do Import Export Business Easily! 36 points excellent video in Hindi

2) Yes, I can do Import Export Business Easily! 36 points excellent video in English

3) Import Export Business – Hindi video

4) Import Export Business - English video

5) Export Import Marathi TV Interview

6) Scope for Commerce Students in International Business- TV Show

7) Scope for Management Student in International Business- TV Show

8) Scope for Engineering Students in International Business – TV Show

9) Women in International Business- TV Show

10) How to do Import Export Business Successfully!‘

11) Where one can get full information on Import Export Business?

12) What to do import & export?

13) Import Export Workshop/ Training/Course/ Diploma

14) How to Start Import Export Business & How to grow it. Live Webinar

15) Success Stories & Failure Stories in Import & Export Business

16) For MSME Scope in Export & Import...

17) Exports In Agri. & Food Products – English & some more videos

18) Exports to Dubai, Aabudhabii. e. UAE

19) Jewelry Exports from India

20) How to attend EXIM workshop to become excellent Exporter

21) Import Export Best Training Course – Online & Offline

22) Agri Product Export

23) Scope for Woman in International Business

24) Management Graduates Scope in International Business

25) Pharma Product's Export

26) Best Import Export Course | Practical Training | Aaronica Global Exim

27) Import Export Business for Commerce Graduates

28) How Do I Get Export Orders? Finding International Buyers

29) What Is APEDA In Import Export Business?

30) Which Is The Best Product To Export From India?

31)EXIM Remark by Manoj Kumar Faridabad

32)EXIM Remarks by Mahesh Telangana

33) What Licenses I Need To Start Import/ Export?

34) How Can I Increase My Import Export Business?

35) Which Is Best B2B Website For Import/Export Business?

36) Export Import Management with Global Marketing

37) How to Start Export Import Business | 51 Points Video

38) Scope for Commerce & Other Graduates in International Business

39)BE A SUCCESSFUL EXPORTER FOR OUR NATION - Marathi video

40) Export of Textile , Cotton, Agri., Food, & other products & services

41) Exports from MP, CG, MH, GJ & CA in Fresh Fruits & Vegetables

42) Exports in Agri. & Food Products- Hindi

43) Start your Online/E-Commerce Business

44) How to Start Export Import Business & Grow it

45) Exports in Textile & Other Products

46) Start and grow EXIM business - Live English Webinar

47)'Import Export Business!' Why, Who, What & How can one do it easily!!

48) Live: Export of Product & Services During & After Lock Down Period

49) Frauds in Import Export Business

50) Import Export for Business Man

51) Import & Export for Women

51) Import & Export for Graduate & Post - Graduate Students

52) Agriculture Exports from India

53) Digital Marketing Setup - Marathi

54)2nd Secret of Successful Businessman

55) Digital Marketing Set up

56) Legal Services Export / Export of Legal Services

57) Export & Import with UAE

58) Service Exports / Exports by Service Providers

59) Import Export Workshop/ Training/Course/ Diploma

60) Exports & Imports with USA

61) Selection on Product for Export

62) Top Products Exported from India

63) What to do import & export?

64)ABMM Career 2 - 'Careers in Business & Industries

65) How to do Import Export Business Successfully!'

66)5 Secrets of Successful Businessman

67) Export from MP, Chhattisgarh & Vidarbha Nagpur

68)EXIM Hindi - Textile & Apparel Export

69)EXIM Hindi - Export Import Practical Training In Delhi, Kolkata, Mumbai and Pune

70) Import Export Business

71) Import Export Business Hindi

72) Import Export Business English video

73) Import Export Business Marathi

74) Women in International Business by Exim Guru Adv. Jayprakash Somani

75) Opportunities in Foreign Trade- Adv. Jayprakash Somani's special interview

• • •

List Of Adv. Jayprakash Somani's Books

1. Supreme Court of India's Leading Case Laws on 'Insolvency & Bankruptcy Code 2016'
2. Bail Matters – Supreme Court's Latest Leading Case Laws
3. Arbitration Matters- Supreme Court's Latest Leading Case Laws
4. Property Matters - Supreme Court's Latest Leading Case Laws
5. Matrimonial Matters- Supreme Court's Latest Leading Case Laws
6. Election Matters- Supreme Court's Latest Leading Case Laws
7. SEBI Matters- Supreme Court's Latest Leading Case Laws
8. Banking Matters- Supreme Court's Latest Leading Case Laws
9. Service Matters- Supreme Court's Latest Leading Case Laws
10. Contempt of Court Matters- Supreme Court's Latest Leading Case Laws
11. Consumer Protection Matters- Supreme Court's Latest Leading Case Laws
12. Corporate Law- Supreme Court's Latest Leading Case Laws
13. Supreme Court's AOR Exam- Leading Cases
14. Armed Force Tribunal - Supreme Court's Latest Leading Case Laws
15. Acquittal From 376 - Supreme Court's Latest Leading Case Laws
16. Negotiable instrument – Supreme Court's Latest Leading Case Laws
17. Contract Act- Supreme Court's Latest Leading Case Laws
18. Insider trading- Supreme Court's Latest Leading Case Laws
19. Foreign Exchange and Management Act- Supreme Court's Latest Leading Case Laws
20. Income Tax Act- Supreme Court's Latest Leading Case Laws
21. Company Law- Supreme Court's Latest Leading Case Laws
22. Competition & Monopoly Matters- Supreme Court's Latest Leading Case Laws

• • •

These Books are available online at

1. **Notion Press:**https://notionpress.com/author/jayprakash_somani
2. **Amazon:**https://www.amazon.in/s?k=jayprakash+somani
3. **Flipkart:**https://www.flipkart.com/search?q=Jayprakash%20Somani

• • •

www.ingramcontent.com/pod-product-compliance
Ingram Content Group UK Ltd.
Pitfield, Milton Keynes, MK11 3LW, UK
UKHW021923190726
13853UKWH00002B/809